SACRAMENTO'S
GOLD RUSH SALOONS

SACRAMENTO'S GOLD RUSH SALOONS

❦ EL DORADO IN A SHOT GLASS ❦

Special Collections of the
Sacramento Public Library

THE
History
PRESS

Published by The History Press
Charleston, SC 29403
www.historypress.net

Front cover, bottom: A bird's-eye view of Sacramento drawn by G.V. Cooper on
December 20, 1849. Captured is the base of J Street along with I, J and K Streets.
Library of Congress.

First published 2014

Manufactured in the United States

ISBN 978.1.62619.170.9

Library of Congress CIP data applied for.

Notice: The information in this book is true and complete to the best of our
knowledge. It is offered without guarantee on the part of the author or The
History Press. The author and The History Press disclaim all liability in
connection with the use of this book.

For my little 49er, Liam.

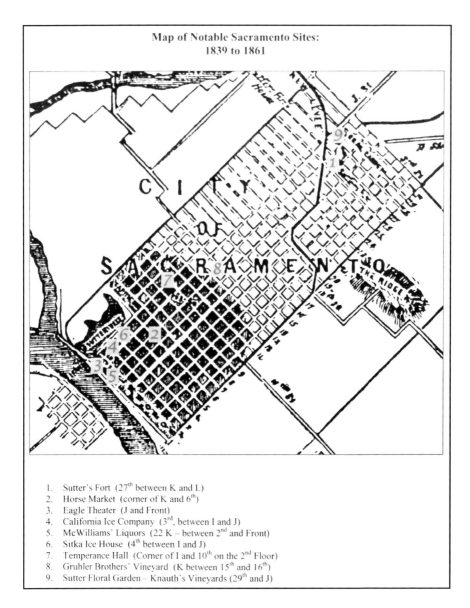

Map of Notable Sacramento Sites:
1839 to 1861

1. Sutter's Fort (27th between K and L)
2. Horse Market (corner of K and 6th)
3. Eagle Theater (J and Front)
4. California Ice Company (3rd, between I and J)
5. McWilliams' Liquors (22 K – between 2nd and Front)
6. Sitka Ice House (4th between I and J)
7. Temperance Hall (Corner of I and 10th on the 2nd Floor)
8. Gruhler Brothers' Vineyard (K between 15th and 16th)
9. Sutter Floral Garden – Knauth's Vineyards (29th and J)

Map of notable Sacramento sites. *Sacramento Public Library.*

CONTENTS

ACKNOWLEDGEMENTS

This book is the culminating effort of various people within the Sacramento Public Library (SPL). Longtime Sacramento Room supervisor Clare Ellis recognized the need for a written work covering the early saloon culture of Sacramento. Current Sacramento Room supervisor Amanda Graham picked up where Ellis left off, providing the ample resources and attention needed to complete the work. Additionally, without the support of SPL director Rivkah Sass, Central Library manager Rebecca Higgerson, Central Library supervisor Roberta Boegel and Library Materials manager Nina Biddle, the book never would have been written. Colleagues, instrumental in proofing and research, were Library Technician Tom Tolley, Library Communications Analyst Linda Beymer, Shelver Betty Miner, Librarian Lori Easterwood and Librarian Kathy Francies.

As with so many Sacramento history endeavors, the Center for Sacramento History stands front and center as a primary contributor with archivists Pat Johnson, Rebecca Crowther and Dylan McDonald brilliantly doing what they do. The same goes for the manager of the California State Library's California History Section, Kathy Correia, and photographic reproduction wizards Katherine Weedman-Cox and Jeff Cox at Cox Black and White Lab Inc.

Finally—and perhaps most importantly—we acknowledge our patrons. It's through their passion and curiosity that we're driven to be the best that we can be. Together, we make the library an irrepressible force for illumination.

Chapter 1
ANTE UP

A walk along modern Sacramento's riverfront takes one through the living, breathing museum of Old Sacramento State Historic Park. Albeit perched some ten to eighteen feet above its original 1849 elevation (it was raised in 1863 to prevent frequent flooding from a quick-to-rise Sacramento River), the district's smattering of cobblestones, boardwalks and false façades conjures forth a bygone era that remains a defining element in the region's identity.

Inextricably tied to the emergence of Sacramento and the city's enduring affection for historical memory is the single most coveted mineral in human history: gold. Few would disagree that James Marshall's 1848 discovery of gold on the American River proved *the* seminal event in the birth and growth of the city. In the find's wake, California would never be the same again. The Gold Rush unleashed a migratory thrust the nation wouldn't see matched until the Dust Bowl and Great Depression of the 1930s. In six months alone, between the winter of 1848 and the spring of 1849, nearly 233 ships, most drunk with Argonauts, sailed through the Golden Gate.[1]

Amid this scene of gold dust dreaming, those who sensed the glint of a different type claimed a hand in the city's fast rise. From riverboat captain to restaurateur to barkeeper, gold was not so much an "x" on the map as it was a thing to be leveraged for profit, a process often referred to as "mining the miner." Among this bevy of incoming merchants were those who would open one of the most enduring standards of nineteenth-century America and the primary focus of this book: the saloon.

A perversion of the French word *salon*, meaning lounge or drawing room, the saloon, according to historian Richard Erdoes, "was often the first substantial building in a new settlement, the last to crumble when it turned into a ghost town."[2] Sacramento was no exception, as indicated by one of the city's first historians, Dr. John Frederick Morse:

> *Long ere San Francisco could boast of a store or hotel that was even decently related to the immense commerce which she concentrated, her public plaza was margined by these saloons, which, in capacity, in bright and glaring illuminations, in gaudy and expensive furniture, would eclipse almost any of the concert, ball, or literary halls in the Atlantic states. And what was true of San Francisco in this particular was true for Sacramento and every other town which achieved importance in the year of '49.*[3]

As soon as Sacramento's Front Street embarcadero was established, a colorful mélange of saloons followed, including the Round Tent, the Humboldt, the Oregon, the El Dorado, the Indian Queen, Lee's Exchange, the Sazerac, the Fashion, the Bank Exchange and the Marion House.

The saloon's existence, both in Sacramento and throughout the West, came with a certain measure of influence. It has been said, tongue-in-cheek, that with the exception of the Battle of the Little Bighorn, all Western history was made within the saloon. If only because it "fueled" so much of the raw bravado and nastiness behind events like the legendary shootout at the O.K. Corral and Sacramento's own lynching of sad Englishman Frederick Roe, the social and historical significance of the saloon is impossible to overstate. Akin to this was the institution's flexible function; while primarily a place for drink and game, it could be much more. As Erdoes notes, in "being all things to all men," the saloon was "an eatery, a hotel, a bath and comfort station, a livery stable, gambling den, dance hall, bordello, barbershop, courtroom, church, social club, political center, dueling ground, post office, sports arena, undertaker's parlor, library, news exchange, theater, opera, city hall, employment agency, museum, trading post, grocery, ice cream parlor."[4]

While seemingly exhaustive, Sacramento would affirm—even add—to such a list. In 1854, Sacramento's Eureka Bath House on Second Street, between I and J, boasted a "splendid bar…furnish[ing] everything in the way of refreshments."[5] Jack's Saloon (owned by Jack Combes), on J and Front Streets, boasted its own shooting gallery that, in 1852, allowed the patron to sip his favorite elixir while also improving his shot. California's very first theater, the Eagle Theater—improvised as it was—was set as an annex to Sacramento's Round Tent Saloon, which opened in the fall of 1849. Some of the city's first town meetings, notably those to discuss the "merits and demerits of the city charter," were held in the St. Louis Exchange, one of Sacramento's original saloons.[6] The reader should be mindful of the saloon as not just a purveyor of vice and refuge, but a real prism of history and viable conduit to affecting a spectrum of changes.

With both their versatility and influence understood, generally speaking, saloons went up for three primary reasons: gaming, drinking and socializing. For so many on the frontier, the lure of gambling was insatiable. Beyond entertainment and raw addiction, gaming meshed well with the frontier's prevailing paradigm of

Dr. John Frederick Morse, recorder of Sacramento's early history and critic of the city's first wave of saloons. *California State Library.*

adventurism and risk-taking. Morse described Sacramento's perilous gambling culture as a "most Herculean grade so far as boldness and amounts hazarded were concerned. Every saloon, every table devoted to betting contingencies was literally crowded and sometimes so completely overwhelmed as to make it physically dangerous to be even a spectator of the scenes. Not one man in ten, if one in twenty, either by his absence or denunciation, condemned the universal mania for gambling which swept the country."[7]

Most considered gambling to be a welcome diversion from the tumult of frontier life, and a talented and wily few, both reviled and revered, viewed it as an actual profession and a viable avenue toward fame and fortune. Gaming legends like the San Francisco–based Charles Cora, a master at faro, and William "Lucky Bill" Thornton, a notorious shell game operator, spent considerable time in Sacramento. What's more, because big players meant big hands, the reported stakes for any number of games seem astonishing, even by today's standards. For one Sacramento poker game, the ante was

$100, while anywhere from $1,000 to $2,500 could be wagered on the best of hands.[8] Speaking on his Gold Rush experience in Sacramento, miner and diarist Peter Decker claimed, "You enter and all is quiet games going on all around you without a word passing thousands of dollars laying [*sic*] on the tables. I have known men to lose $2,000 in an evening."[9]

The history of the American West, distilled into popularity through film, literature and metaphor, would indicate that poker was *the* game; not so in antebellum Sacramento. At least in the early going, monte, faro and thimblerig ruled the day. Monte (or Tiger) was an import, finding its way to California from Spain via Mexico. By way of its Iberian origins, the game also was known as Spanish monte and played with a special forty-card deck with the following suits: clubs, swords, suns and cops. Like the more modern game of blackjack, or "21," players went against the dealer. Accordingly, the dealer would turn up two cards and then a third from the deck. Players then bet on whether the third card, or "gate," matched either one of the first two. As historian Mark Eifler states, "The game was regarded as one in which it was easy for a dealer to cheat a player, resembling a shell game."[10] For this reason, games played against a dealer and/or operated by the house were referred to as "banking games" and would eventually be outlawed.

Faro, or "Buck the Tiger," also a banking game, was viewed as a prestige game and was popular—not simply because of the spectacle it offered the onlooker, but because it was known to give the player an almost even shot against the dealer.[11] Its birth goes back to eighteenth-century France, while its name, derived from "pharaoh" or "pharo," refers to the French reference to the King of Hearts as the pharaoh.[12] Only card values, dealt from a fifty-two-card deck, were considered, thus making suits irrelevant. After the first card was exposed and discarded, twenty-five two-card pairs were laid out, leaving one unplayed card. The player would bet against the dealer, who drew two cards from the deck for each "turn." Hands were decided when the player then placed a bet on the card he thought would win.

Thimblerig, known also as "the shell game," was perhaps the most elementary of the early gambling diversions. With origins going back to ancient Egypt, it involved the bettor choosing which of three shells contained a pea. Despite the prospects of a one-in-three chance for victory, it was far from a sure thing, for as we will see, thimblerig acquired its dubious suffix for a reason.

Poker was born in the late 1700s in New Orleans and was perhaps named after a similar German game called Pochen or Poch. In its original, pre-1850 form, the game used a twenty-card deck. However, as the country

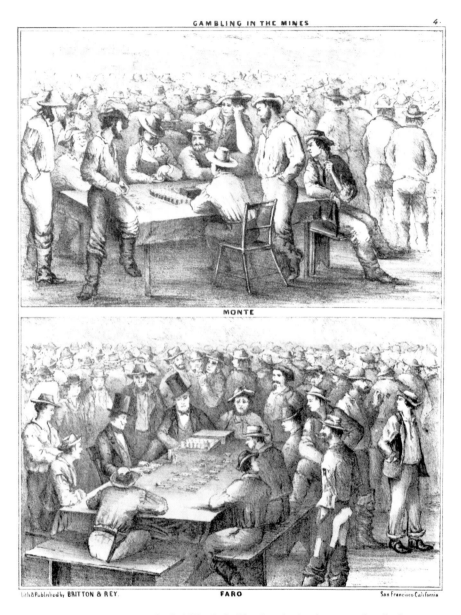

The gamble was ever present in Gold Rush California, whether in wet or dry diggings or at the monte or faro tables. *Center for Sacramento History*.

pushed west, so too did the number of cards in play, as thirty-two were added for a total of fifty-two. Unlike monte, it demanded no permanent dealer, and quite unlike roulette, it required skill, both in reading the odds of one's cards and the tenor of an opponent's expression. The game, from beginning to end, was seductively easy: based on a random deal, the player with the highest hand—typically consisting of five cards—won the pot. Poker also was fast and could be played by as few as two or as many as ten. As Morse put it, poker "was a great game; although it was not so popular as a public betting medium, yet it was the test scene of the mightiest hazards then made."[13] Sustaining poker was not just its simplicity, but its status as a non-banking game. Near the end of the 1850s, when monte, faro and other house-controlled games were falling to the law, poker found its legs, eventually taking its place as Young America's tacit—if not official—game of chance for decades to come.

By mid-century, alcohol consumption was also reaching new heights of popularity in all of American society. As historian Elliot West states, one could expect to see, in the nineteenth century, "as much as ten gallons of pure alcohol per year for every adult American, according to one estimate."[14] In the West, the level of drink's appeal meant that one saloon could be found for every 50 to 100 persons.[15] Placing Sacramento into a similar context, in 1851, it contained 7,000 residents, or 77 citizens for every establishment licensed to sell alcohol.[16] While it is true that early Sacramentans, from miner to merchant, enjoyed drink, some of the more high-profile figures in town were more than equal to the task, as evidenced in the December 17, 1850 *Sacramento Transcript*, which states, "A New Species of Drunkenness—The *Sacramento Transcript*, in speaking of a soiree given by the Mayor (Horace Smith), says: 'The Mayor of the city, the ladies, &c., were appropriately and elegantly drunk.'"[17]

There were a puritanical few, however, who sought a dry California. The goal was simple: halt the excessive consumption of alcohol and prevent a litany of consequential social problems such as poverty, crime, domestic tumult, hooliganism and immorality. Despite its youth, by late 1850, Sacramento possessed various temperance groups, with the Sons of Temperance, Pacific Star Chapter, being the oldest. With its original office located at 409 J Street, the sons maintained a close eye on the city's saloon district, most of which covered the corridor from Front Street through Seventh Street.

The city also boasted no fewer than seven temperance-friendly churches. One, the so-called Baptist Chapel, encouraged citizens in the June 6, 1850 *Sacramento Transcript* to help assemble a "temperance organization." The announcement continues to mention, and not absent a tone of moral entitlement, that "several speeches were expected and by representations made to us by those who know, persons who go will be treated, not with liquor, but with eloquence and intellect."[18]

In 1839, John Sutter founded Sutter's Fort. It was there that he established brewing and distilling facilities. *Sacramento Public Library*.

In the first few years of the 1850s, the sons and, later, the Woman's Christian Temperance Union pressed for restrictions on Sacramento saloons, marching in full regalia on July 4, 1851, to promote their righteous cause. Even the region's first record of news, the *Placer Times*, displayed some modicum of temperance tendency, impishly reprinting in 1848 a *New York Tribune* mention of Captain John Sutter's loss in the California gubernatorial election coming as a result of his being a "drinking man." It goes on to note, "If this be so, it speaks well for California and places her considerably in advance of some of the older states."[19] As we will see, such moral suasion did little to affect a mostly male Sacramento population, whose demands for the saloon as both drinking place and social hub could not be denied.

Also worthy of mention is Sacramento's placement in one of the world's most lush agricultural regions, where all the raw material for drink was provided. Early on, the eye-popping size of even the most pedestrian crops made it into local newsprint. "Another Mammoth Melon," "Enormous," "Large Beet," "Monster Melon" and "Huge Potatoes" were just a few of the more amusing headlines, but none could top that from September 5, 1854, in the *Democratic Journal*, which read "Siamese Watermelon."[20] The watermelon of note, grown in the garden of John Denn, was on display at the city's Union Saloon, located at J and Third Streets. Coined a "most wonderful curiosity," the melon was reported to weigh only twenty pounds, but having "united and formed one" from two melons, it conjured forth ample curiosity.[21] The value of such agricultural riches was far from lost on locals, whose emerging confidence was evident in this passage from the *Sacramento Daily Union* in 1858, speaking to America's mid-century standard in the distilled spirit: "We need not send to England for English Ale, or to Scotland or Ireland for Scotch or Irish whiskey…it will distill at our very doors, in the quality of any national liquor we may call for."[22] With wheat, barley, hops and various other flora in rich abundance and within easy reach to a vanguard of brewers, vintners and distillers, the city's saloons would come to expect both high reliability and quality out of local alcohol production. This was especially true for the local production of flavorful English ales of the day that were highly susceptible to spoilage, thus making transport from the east out of the question. Sacramento would also see the emergence of the more effervescent and durable Teutonic-style lagers, thanks primarily to the spoil-resistant yeasts that were imported to North America by German immigrants in the 1840s.

The early American West's unique frontier zeitgeist stood as an additional factor in the saloon's rise. The West was not for everyone; life was hard and wickedly unforgiving. As was aptly stated in the August 11, 1849 *Placer Times*, those coming to California for the mining experience "should bear in mind that in California there is yet no law, but the will of the strongest and that life and property are insecure and that in the most favorable of circumstances, they must labor harder and fare [*sic*] worse than our Southern slaves, or state prison convicts. Then again, the climate is unhealthy. We dislike to be the prophet of evil, but we cannot forebear expressing the opinion that of those who go out to California, but few will return and that those few will not be much richer than before."[23]

While not always the safest of spots, the saloon filled a void of insecurity and loneliness for untold numbers of people whose lives were susceptible to a unique type of angst. The effect of missed wives and families, the boredom of life in a virtual cultural/entertainment vacuum and the exhaustion that came with tearing through dry diggings one day and standing for hours in the most frigid of mountain streams the next all added up. This collective momentum of deprivation fomented a hearty thirst and, with that, demands for a place to quench that thirst.

It also bears mention that saloonists enjoyed access to a male-dominated market with a community of parched miners, impulsive adolescents and dusty frontiersman, all of whom were members of the gender that drank the vast majority of alcohol being consumed in nineteenth-century America.[24] Accordingly, the 1850 census reveals the starkness of this gender disparity as it notes that 72 percent of the state's population was between the ages of twenty and forty and that 92 percent of California's total population was male.[25]

It's within this colorful context that we consider various questions regarding saloon culture in early Sacramento. What were the city's first and most notable saloons? Who established them? Who used them? From which vineyards, breweries and distilleries did they obtain their alcohol? And finally, what were the biggest threats to their existence, both manmade and natural? In addressing as much, we'll attempt to construct a cohesive historical narrative, the extent of which will stretch from the area's earliest European origins through the Gold Rush and near the early rumblings of the American Civil War.

Chapter 2
HAVE FORT OR TENT, WILL DEBAUCH: 1846—49

To determine Sacramento's first saloon, it's best to consider geography. Based on what a dearth of primary sources tells us, the *city* of Sacramento possesses one clear winner. If we consider the *greater area* where the American River meets the Sacramento River, we look no further than venerable Sutter's Fort, located today on a grassy knoll between Twenty-sixth and Twenty-eighth Streets and K and L Streets.

By most accounts, the first saloon in the city of Sacramento was as makeshift as they come: a few posts, some rope and a wind sail, offering "poor whiskey and poorer entertainment."[26] The Stinking Tent, as it grew to be known, was described by Morse as "the first place of gaming in this city…situated in 'J' Street between Second and Third, the present site of the Diana."[27] It was operated by James Lee, known through some sources as "Jimmie" Lee. Monte was the predominant game, and its distinction as the first gambling saloon in the city gives it obvious significance.[28] An anonymously authored lithograph portraying Sacramento in July 1849 reveals an establishment located roughly between Second and Third Streets, and on J, called the "Big Tent."[29] Adorned with flags and gaudy capital letters spelling out its name, it is likely that this was nothing more than sanitization of the more amusing Stinking Tent.

If we consider Sacramento proper to be our delimiter—looking east from Front Street to Twentieth Street—the Stinking Tent is it. However, reports that predate Morse point to Sutter's Fort as the region's first place of gaming and drink. William Robinson Grimshaw arrived in Sacramento in

An 1848 rendering of Sacramento's J Street with the Big Tent in the upper section of the image. *California State Library.*

October 1848 to clerk for commercial dynamo Sam Brannan. Grimshaw's reminiscences, written between 1848 and 1850, provide us with a taste of life at Fort Sutter, including its sundry entertainments. Insofar as gaming and drink in what appears to be late 1848, he states, "In the centre of the inside of the fort was a two story abode building, still standing, lower portion of which was used as a barroom with a monte table or two in it. This bar was crowded with customers night and day and never closed from one month's end to the other."[30] Thompson and West's definitive 1880 history of Sacramento County paints a somewhat similar picture of the Fort's central building: "The front room [on the first floor] was used for drinking and gambling purposes…the bar was kept open night and day."[31] Gold dust proved to be the preferred payment in the bar as the miner "opened his purse and the barkeeper took a pinch of gold dust, the extent of the pinch being regulated by the quality and quantity of the liquor consumed."[32]

This barroom was likely under the operation of one Peter Slater, a native of Independence, Missouri; a Mormon; a widower; and a father of nine children. According to historian Laura T. Collins, Slater "made a fortune in the vending of drinks in this room—considering the price of fifty cents for a tablespoonful, $35.00 for a quart of brandy or whiskey."[33] Although not

Right: William Robinson Grimshaw, a clerk at Sutter's Fort, provides one of the earliest descriptions of the structure's saloon. *California State Library*.

Below: This circa 1880 photograph shows Fort Sutter's central building, home to Parly Slater's saloon. *Sacramento Public Library*.

much is known of Slater, one of our most revealing descriptions of the man comes from Swiss immigrant and fort clerk Heinrich Lienhard. He recounts Slater's running a bowling alley and selling food and assorted drinks at the Fort. He goes on to say, "Slater, who was not at all like his countrymen, seemed to have a fine character; he was a handsome, thoughtful, modest man who never harbored any ill will or tried to harm anyone. Many times I went to his store when I did not care to bowl or drink; he was always friendly and we often chatted together."[34] Lienhard "was favorably impressed by [Slater]; he seemed like a level-headed, sober and sensible man, the type who would not sacrifice principles for more gold."

It is likely that this is the same Slater who, in the spring the 1849, ran and was elected to the city's board of commissioners and the same man who, according to Sacramento Superior Court records, went on to run a ferry over the American River prior to dying of an indeterminable illness in December 1849. We also know that, at the time of his death, Slater's personal property, appropriately enough, consisted partly of "242 three-quarter ounces of gold dust," not to mention three dozen bottles of India Pale Ale.[35]

Underlining the presence of a fort saloon was Sutter's immense fondness for drink. One Swiss visitor, Theophile de Rutte, recounted that during Sutter's run for the governorship of California, he and others enjoyed a "bender" with the captain, lasting for "10 days and nights" and accounting for $11,500 in "champagne, fine wines and strong liquor."[36] De Rutte also mentions Sutter's decision to situate his campaign headquarters in the basement of the Hotel de France (Sutter was an avid Francophile), where, of course, there was an open bar.

Lienhard was acquainted with Sutter through his work at the Fort. The former's somewhat amusing testimony regarding Sutter's penchant for alcohol follows:

> *I had no idea* [Sutter] *drank as much as he did. Soon I had an opportunity to become better acquainted with his habits and it was during my second week at the fort, I believe, that I saw him walking with an unsteady, swaying motion which left no doubt as to his condition…I learned from acquaintances, who had known Sutter for longer time and more intimately, that he was often intoxicated.*[37]

Sutter naturally made sure that the fort contained a distillery and brewery, or what Heinrich Kuenzel coined "Brauerei u. Brennerei" in his 1849 map of the fort. Used between 1844 and 1846 and standing two stories in height (roughly sixty feet by twenty-five feet), the distillery was fed with grapes picked by Sutter's Nisenan and Kanaka slaves along the area's lush riverbanks and wetlands.[38] The pickings were mashed and fermented into whiskey barrels, with the mash then being distilled into brandy. According to archaeological digs done between 1950 and 1960, the compound may have contained up to four stills. Operations were halted, however, as a result of Sutter's inability to keep the understandably popular elixir safe from several fort inhabitants and a handful of area natives.[39]

Sacramento's first brewery, established in the early spring of 1849, was located adjacent to Fort Sutter, just at the corner of M and Twenty-eighth Streets. As stated in a *Placer Times* advertisement, "P. Cadel and Company" boasted "the best quality of Ale and Beer."[10] The brewery's founder, Peter Cadel, was from Baden, Germany, having settled in Sacramento in 1846, originally as a dairyman in Sutterville. Traveler J. Goldsborough Bruff provided an account in December 1850 of Cadel's new brewery in stating that "within a few hundred yards of the [Sacramento Hospital] are several neat frame houses, one of which is a brewery, with a sign of 'Galena Brewery'[11] on it. We tested their ale and found it good," with each glass priced at twenty-five cents.

German-born Heinrich Lienhard had a lot to say about John Sutter's drinking habits and the haphazard prospects of gambling in early California. *California State Library*.

Cadel's ales appear to have been the first of their kind brewed in the Sacramento area. Fermented rapidly via top-fermentation yeasts and at a high temperature (sixty to seventy-five degrees Fahrenheit), the natural sugar content remained unchanged, preserving a certain sweetness not found in lagers, which were made by bottom-fermentation yeasts and brewed for a longer period and at a cooler temperature. A notable figure in the spread of ale-style drinks in early Sacramento was Scotsman Thomas W. Legget, who established a public house of his own, Legget's Ale House, on 42 Front Street in November 1852. He also operated the "No. 2 ale cellar" or "Branch No. 2" at 87 K Street. It has been said that Legget enticed customers by saying, "There's many an idea in a barrel of ale. Billie Shakespeare and Bobbie Burns didn't drink for nothing."[12]

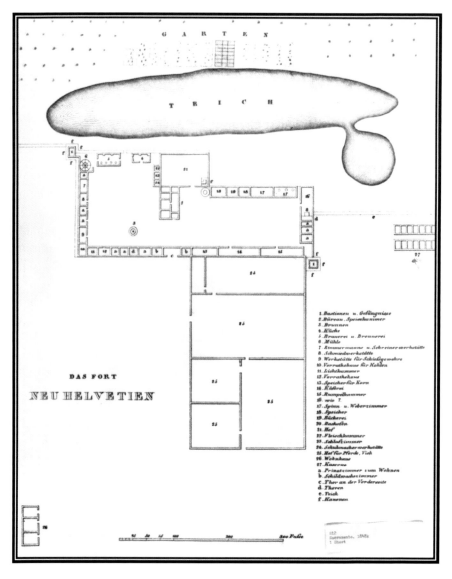

Kuenzel's 1849 map of Sutter's Fort. Brewery and distilling facilities were located in the fort's northwest corner, near the blockhouse. *California State Library.*

Cadel decided to rent out the brewery in 1853 and then sold it to Philip Scheld for $2,000 in 1854. Under the new leadership, the operation became known as the Sacramento Brewery. Also a German, Scheld immigrated to America in 1845. Once in his hands, the brewery would flourish for the next three decades. As of 1860, it was two stories high, made of brick and

LEGGET'S
PIONEER
LIQUOR WAREHOUSE,

No. 42 Front Street, between J and K,
(OPPOSITE STEAMBOAT LANDING,)

ALSO,

BRANCH, 87 K St., bet. Third and Fourth,

SACRAMENTO.

The undersigned, having arrangements whereby he is in regular receipt of

ENGLISH ALE and PORTER,

The Trade may rely upon procuring

A SUPERIOR ARTICLE,

WHICH, TOGETHER WITH

WINES, LIQUORS, CORDIALS, &c.

Of all kinds, are offered at the very

LOWEST CASH RATES.

Thankful for the very liberal patronage heretofore extended, he trusts, by unremitting attention, to merit a continuance of the same.

T. W. LEGGET,
PROPRIETOR.

An advertisement from the 1856 *City Directory* for Thomas Leggett's ale business, one of Sacramento's earliest alcohol retailers. *Sacramento Public Library*.

Primeval Sutter's Fort, the location of some of California's earliest breweries. *Center for Sacramento History*.

possessed a basement for cooling and storage. At 120 feet long and 100 feet wide, it was large enough to cover two lots and, according to one source, was producing some 700 gallons of lager per day by 1855. Scheld's fuel to burn, per round of brewing, included twenty-five thousand pounds of malt and three thousand pounds of barley, while the machinery running the brewery included both horsepower for the malt mill and a windmill for the use of water. As of 1858, Scheld was making an average of 3,500 gallons of beer per week, with distribution to nearly thirty saloons throughout the city.[13]

As mentioned earlier, the rise of area beer production did so under the most ideal of conditions. Between 1850 and 1860, barley production rose sharply from roughly 3,000 bushels to just over 514,000 bushels, making Sacramento County the leading barley producer in the state for the latter year.[14] Yolo County's strain of barley followed in similar fashion, "particularly on the banks of Cache Creek," and was referred to by the *Union* as a most "precocious grain." By 1858, the city's breweries were consuming 502 tons of barley a year in the production of beer.[15] As for hops, they grew aplenty near present-day Sacramento State University. Originally known as Brighton, at mid-century, the area contained California's most extensive hops fields.[16] An additional source of seed and grains was Smith's Pomological Gardens and Nursery. Founded by A.P. (Anthony) Smith in 1849, the gardens were located just north of the present-day East Sacramento district of Sacramento but south of the American River. Smith produced fruit and vegetable seeds from his fifty-

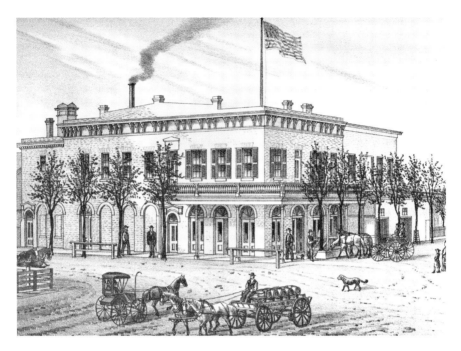

The Sacramento Brewery, opened by Peter Cadel, was the city's first known brewery specializing in ales. *Sacramento Public Library*.

acre site that, in spite of being attacked by a "plague of locusts" in the summer of 1855, had doubled in size by 1858.[17]

There were other factors enhancing Sacramento's ability to brew. The allure of the Gold Rush, coupled with the failed European Revolutions of 1848, created a stream of immigrants, particularly Germans and Frenchmen, who possessed a near-biological acumen for beer production. The presence of Irishmen, searching for gold while also fleeing moribund economic conditions in their own country after 1840, further increased the supply of knowledgeable beer makers. A quick scan of 1850's census reveals not more than six individuals claiming to be brewers.[18] Three were German, two were from Massachusetts and one was French. The Frenchman, George Zins, and one of the Germans, George Weiser, collaborated in 1850 to construct their own brewery at Twenty-ninth and J.

Other early Sacramento brewers of European origin were the Germanic Schildknecht and Koester, whose names appear in the 1851 *Directory*.[19] According to the publication, their brewery would have been situated on Front Street, between F and G (also referred to as Sacramento and Broad, respectively).

Although short-lived, another business, the United States Brewery, was located on K Street, between Eighth and Ninth in the summer of 1851. It produced ale, as it claimed, with an "excellence and cheapness unsurpassed."[50]

Possessing more of a muted presence was wine, whose California genesis rests in the cultivation—by early Spanish missions—of grapes for the creation of the symbolic blood of Christ for the Eucharistic liturgy, a process that dates back to the arrival in California of Catholic missionaries in the late seventeenth century. As for Sacramento, an advertisement in the March 19, 1851 *Transcript* declares, "GRAPE CUTTINGS!! GRAPE CUTTINGS!! from the celebrated Vineyard of William Wolfskill for sale."[51] Another entry in the October 3, 1850 *Transcript* hails the $25,000 harvest from General Vallejo's Sonoma vineyard, a parcel of land covering not more than an acre.[52] Even Captain Sutter, in an attempt to vault his way out of debt, advertised the sale of his prized vines at Hock Farm. Akin to the production of beer, all boded well for the growth of Central Valley viticulture, and by 1853, California would become the leading producer of wine in the country at 58,055 gallons per year.[53]

Now that we have explored one element that brought saloons to Sacramento and kept them there, let us take a look beyond Slater's barroom or the Stinking Tent and at some of the city's other drinking spots. One dispatch from an unknown 49er provides a glimpse of the city's gambling and drinking culture in December 1850: "Sacramento is the liveliest place I ever saw…about every tent is a gambling house and it made my head swim to see money flying around."[54] Another superb depiction comes from *New York Tribune* journalist Bayard Taylor, whose travels throughout the West yielded a treasure-trove of cultural description. He states, "Sacramento City was one place by day and another by night; and of the two, its night side was the peculiar."[55] He adds that as a miner made his way through nocturnal Sacramento, there was the following to see:

> *In the more frequented streets, where drinking and gambling had full swing, there was a partial light, streaming out through doors and crimson window-curtains, to guide his steps.*
>
> *The door of many a gambling-hell on the levee…stands invitingly open; the wail of torture from innumerable musical instruments peals from all quarters through the fog and darkness.*
>
> *The gentleman who played the flute in the next room to yours at home has been hired at an ounce a night (gold dust) to perform in the drinking-tent across the way.*[56]

Well-traveled journalist Bayard Taylor provided some of the first descriptions of Sacramento's early Ersatz-style saloons. *Library of Congress.*

The most famous and versatile of this next generation of saloons was the Round Tent. Established in late July 1849, "first on J between Front and Second streets and afterwards on Front between I and J," the saloon could claim direct lineage to the Stinking Tent.[57] As Richard DeArment states, "A group of sharpers took over [Lee's] Stinking Tent, changing the name to the Round Tent."[58] Those "sharpers" were Zaddock Hubbard and Gates Brown. From its inception, the Round Tent was a gaming mecca. As a young miner, William Johnston's view of Sacramento's "one great gambling rendezvous" matched that of "a circus-like affair of mammoth proportions, capable of accommodating one hundred or more persons."[59] Morse's take on the Tent is a bit less complimentary:

> *Music and a decorated bar and obscene pictures were the great attractions that lined this whirlpool of fortune and coerced into the vortex of penury and disgrace many an American who had come to California without his morals or the decencies which he was taught at home...toilers of the country, including traders, mechanics, miners and speculators, lawyers, doctors and ministers, concentrated at this gambling focus like flying insects around a lighted candle at night; and like such insects seldom left the delusive glare until scorched and consumed by the watch fires of destruction.*[60]

While Morse, generally thin on the establishment's physical description, recounts the Tent's being fifty feet in diameter, Johnston tells us that the "interior revealed two large tables at which the Mexican game of monte

This early rendering of Front Street, between I and J Streets, features both the Eagle Theater and the Round Tent Saloon. *Center for Sacramento History.*

was being played."[61] He also describes ornate roulette tables, accompanied by bankers "with pleasant, smiling heaps of gold and silver beside them, so arranged to be enticing to their expecting customers."[62] Johnston goes on to paint the bar area as a "conspicuous feature…decorated with large and costly mirrors, behind shelves adorned with a glittery array of decanters containing sparkling liquors…there were extraordinary pyramids of lemons, towering peaks of Havana cigars and gorgeous vases containing peppermint. A bevy of patrons thronged this attractive bar and there was a constant clicking of glasses, popping of corks, amid the gurgling sound of tut, tut, tut, etc., etc., etc."[63]

In 1850, miner William Swain described the Round Tent as "a place made of a huge circular tent, like a small circus and emblazoned with large letters 'City Diggins.' This during the day is almost unoccupied, but at night music rings out and it is to excess crowded."[64] Vouching Swain's claim is a short entry in the *Placer Times* in October 1849 that describes performances by the California Ethiopian Serenaders at the tent "to full houses and much to the amusement of people generally."[65]

The Round Tent's outward appearance was as follows: the base was rounded, while the sides rose from dirt floors to a pointed crescendo, which was topped off with a flag. This profile's source is George Victor Cooper's 1849 lithograph, a valuable tool for pinpointing several key landmarks in early Sacramento. An additional description of the Tent comes from miner William Redmond Ryan, who recalled the tent to be "thirty feet in diameter, by twenty-five in height, from the conical top of which floats a large red flag inscribed with the words 'Miner's Exchange.'"[66] Ryan also recounts six

Early Sacramento contractor Albion Sweetser very likely manufactured the Round Tent Saloon and its attachment to the Eagle Theater. *California State Library*.

or eight large gambling tables, "each…let out at the nightly rental of twelve dollars." The Tent's bar was positioned "opposite the door, where large profits are realized upon refreshments sold to the players and strangers." Insofar as a builder, "it is probable that [Albion C.] Sweetser… constructed the long-remembered 'Round Tent.'" Sweetser was a native of Maine and became known for doing some of the earliest professional designing and building in the California territory, one method being the use of "willow poles for structural parts and canvas and tarred paper for roofing and wall coverings."[67] It's ironic, however, that the builder of one of the city's most notorious drinking and gaming spots was also an ardent teetotaler.

A true legend of the Round Tent was Lucky Bill Thornton (also referred to in some sources as Thorington). A native of New York State, Thornton jumped a California-bound wagon train in the late 1840s. Deposited in Sacramento, Thornton would come to choose none other than the Round Tent to introduce to the river city his specialty: the shell game. Lying in wait, he positioned himself in squat near the entrance to the Round Tent, where laid out before him was a sleek board and three halved walnut shells. With the charm of a cavalier and wielding an uncanny sleight of hand, Bill worked wonders. His "Lucky" sobriquet proved a total misnomer, however, as he was an unrepentant cheater. In addition to the cork-shaped pea, seemingly the only one visible to players, he maintained an additional pea under a nail on one of his swiftly moving fingers. The trickster would release his duplicate pea whenever needed to negate an "on the square" selection. Bill also used "cappers," gamblers who were planted to "win" on occasion, so as to lure wide-eyed neophytes. So effective was Thornton's charade that, in just a few months, he was able to extract $24,000 from the good people of

G.V. Cooper's 1849 lithograph provides a choice view of the Eagle Theater, the tip of the Round Tent Saloon (E). *Library of Congress.*

Sacramento.[68] Because his heavy addiction to faro, penchant for pretty girls and prodigious spending habits demanded that Bill keep producing gaudy sums, he was forced to seek fortunes elsewhere.

Music was a standard saloon offering, or in the case of the Tent, a "noticeable feature" of a "modest string band seated on an elevated bench; the forerunner of those great orchestras which but a few months later became so marked a feature in the gambling saloons of California."[69] Hubbard and Brown would come to follow the lead of many East Coast saloons by introducing live theater. The concept of the "concert saloon" was likely born out of a similar movement that sprang out of England in the late 1840s. The primary goal was to keep patrons in a drinking mood by the expansion of entertainment options, which ranged from theatrical skits and magic shows to circus-type acts.

Once the Round Tent resolved to go forth with the "concert saloon" model, the Eagle Theater was born. Not only would the Eagle be the first public building in Sacramento, but as of July 1849, it also claimed distinction as California's first theater. Situated on the corner of J and Front Streets and constructed with a patchwork of materials—wood, canvas and tin—the Eagle was large. According to historian Charles Hume, it could hold up to three hundred patrons, with its overall dimensions being some seventy-five feet by twenty-six feet in size. It also possessed a balcony area that could hold from sixty to seventy people.[70] Entry to the theater, by most accounts, seems to have come via the saloon section of the Round Tent, where tickets would have been purchased at the bar, while actors' dressing rooms were constructed out of the "packing boxes that transported the bar and trappings of the Round Tent Saloon."[71] The Eagle also seems to have possessed a saloon area of its own, accessible from the Front Street side of the theater.

When the theater opened for dance and choir performances in late September, the *Placer Times* declared, "In the main, the Eagle Theatre is all we may look for under the circumstances and as a respectable place of amusement, is entitled to the 'full blast' of amusement."[72] Despite its early successes, the theater quickly slipped into financial trouble. Attendance ebbed, with creditors eventually forcing Hubbard to cede "the saloon building in front of the…theatre with the entire stock of liquors, furniture and fixtures thereto belonging with the lease for the ground on which said saloon stands reserving to the said theatre the right of entrance through said

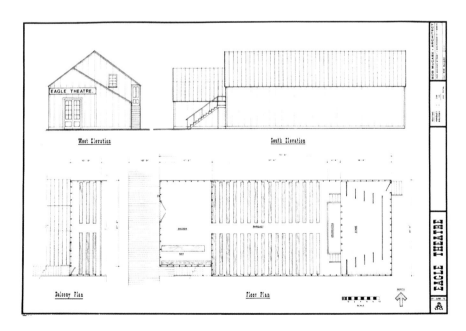

Elevations of California's first theater and eventual concert saloon, the Eagle Theater, located at Front and J Streets. *Center for Sacramento History*.

saloon to theatre."[73] Exacerbating Hubbard's travails was severe illness, so dire that official records from Sacramento's Court of First Instance describe "Mr. Hubbard not being in his right mind."[74] With Hubbard gone by the end of October, the theater was sold to S. Clinton Hastings and Samuel Bruce, with William Hargrove assuming ownership of the Round Tent for the price of $4,075.

The resulting inventory of the theater and saloon's contents provides an interesting window into the Eagle and Tent: two mirrors, one clock, ten decanters, two dozen goblets, four dozen wine glasses, two dozen cordials, one can of peaches, one dozen mugs, one bottle of bitters, fifteen gallons of brandy, twenty gallons of liquor, six chandeliers, two small mirrors, one iron safe, twenty-one lamps, one gold scale, two tables, one dozen plates, one dozen soup plates, four settees (sofas), one box of raisins, one dozen cans of peas and one set of scenery.[75] An additional list of items, purchased from Jones and Company for $309 by Hubbard, Brown and Company but never paid for, included thirty-eight gallons of gin, three large dishes, two dozen oysters and one thousand cigars, spelled "sigars" in the legal record.[76] We also know from county court records that the barkeepers at the Round Tent were paid roughly $12 a day for their services.

With the movement of the Eagle from Front to Second and then taking on the name of the Tehama, did its saloon simply go away? The physical nature of both the Round Tent and the Stinking Tent made it easy for proprietors to literally fold up shop and speedily move to a new location. Giving credence to the Tent's living well into 1850 was this from the August 13 *Sacramento Transcript*: "OLD ROUND TENT—The proprietors will sell the above tent and fixtures at a reasonable rate, as they intend to leave soon. The Old Round Tent is so well known, commendation is unnecessary. Those who wish to purchase will do well to call soon. BAKER & WEEKES."[77] The Tent's run had ended. The competition, something that the saloon worried little about at first, had become a factor.

Hubbard's efforts with the Tent were meaningful. In spite of a sporadic lifespan, the Round Tent and the Eagle fit the loose definition of a modern-day casino, offering gambling, drink, food and onstage entertainment. Moreover, from a cultural standpoint, Hume includes an important point in understanding the market demands for a place like the Eagle: "The audiences of this early theater were not ignorant boobies who might appreciate anything put on the boards, but instead were men who were used to attending the theater at home and were anxious to resume the cultural experiences that they had left behind."[78]

The Tent's allure also served as a cultural nexus for the Gold Rush's varied nations and races as, in Johnston's words, it drew "various nationalities…noticeable on account of peculiarities of dress," which included "beside those whom we call Americans: Mexicans and native Californians, men from many of the South American States and from numerous islands of the Pacific."[79] One Englishman had much to say about the city's diverse gaming clientele: "The most mixed and motley congregations, white, half-castes, copper, mahogany and black." He continues, "The cloaked Spaniard and the phlegmatic German laid down their stakes and stood back from the circle, revealing nothing. The Chinese were the most innocent-looking and the best gamblers. Their bland and baby-like faces looked serene, win or lose."[80]

An inventory of the City Hospital wards in the winter of 1850 further shows the increasingly diverse racial and ethnic flavor of the entire city: "6 English, 1 Switzerland, 1 Wales, 1 India, 1 Australia, 2 Holland, 3 Belgium, 1 Azores, 1 Holstein, 7 France, 19 Ireland, 1 Sandwich Islands, 1 Sweden, 1 Norway, 2 New South Wales, 1 Singapore, 5 Mexico, 2 Hungary, 6 Scotland, 17 Germany, 479 United States."[81]

The Tent as a congress of multiple cultures is a fascinating one. Outside the mines, it is difficult to think of any other place where this kind of integration could have occurred. While racism was indeed prevalent and exacerbated by inevitable gold field jealousies, the saloon at least forced the races to commingle and interact within a simple social setting. This alone makes the Tent's role—as well as that of the general saloon—in Sacramento's social evolution a significant one.

What happened to the man who gave birth to the Tent and Eagle? Hubbard attempted to open a type of eatery/saloon called "Hubbard's Exchange," located on Front Street between K and L Streets. The June 6, 1850 *Sacramento Transcript* was the first to get word out: "This establishment has been newly refitted under the superintendence of the old proprietor, Mr. Hubbard, who will be glad to visit with friends and assures them they will find the very best liquors and attentive attendants."[82] However, not long after opening, the enterprise went under, as did another chapter in Hubbard's moribund business career.

Lucky Bill, who couldn't fight the allure of so many naïve miners peppering the Mother Lode, left Sacramento in 1851. In and out of trouble and California for the next few years, Thornton eventually went clean, settling in Nevada's Carson Valley near the town of Genoa. There, he found prosperity and respect through the operation of a ranch that was fitted with several thousand head of cattle. Unfortunately for Thornton,

This twentieth-century rendering of the Round Tent Saloon was done by Sacramento historian Ted Baggelmann. *Sacramento Public Library*.

old habits fell hard. For crimes of murder and cattle theft, he found his ultimate demise at the end of a hangman's noose in June 1858. It is said that in facing his impending execution, Thornton spoke these final, cool words: "Gentlemen, your executioner seems nervous. Permit me to put the noose around my own neck."[83]

In spite of being dominated by the Round Tent, other saloons broke into the Sacramento market, primarily along the western end of J Street. Two such places, the Plains and the Shades, were mentioned by news writer W.A. George in a February 12, 1850 dispatch to the *Missouri Republican* as two of Sacramento's "many gambling houses."[84] Hubert Bancroft described the Plains as fittingly adorning its walls "with scenic illustrations of the route across the continent."[85] Bayard Taylor described the extensive mural:

> *Some Western artist, who came across the country, adorned its walls with scenic illustrations of the route, such as Independence Rock, the Sweet-Water Valley, Fort Laramie, Wind River Mountains, etc. There was one of a pass in the Sierra Nevada, on the Carson River route. A wagon and team were represented as coming down the side of a hill, so nearly perpendicular that it seemed no earthly power could prevent them from making but a single fall from the summit to the valley. These particular oxen, however, were*

happily independent of gravitation and whisked their tails in the face of the zenith, as they marched slowly down.[86]

The Shades' identity as a Sacramento saloon is an elusive one. Its sole mention appears in the July 20, 1849 *Placer Times*, which, in extolling the growth of Sacramento, stated, "You may purchase your breakfast at the Washington market, dine at Sweeny's and drink your glass at the Shades."[87]

If the appearance of every "golden age" requires an usher, the collective spirit of Sutter's Fort, the Stinking Tent, the Round Tent and various others proved to be that very thing for Sacramento and the saloon. Each of these early establishments created an identity of escape and leisure that, when set against the backdrop of an infantile frontier town and a near-pathological grab for gold, merely set the stage for so much more to come.

Chapter 3
GIVE US YOUR GREEDY, GREEN AND LONELY: 1850—52

By early 1850, the heart of Sacramento's saloon "district" was settling in near the intersection of Front and J Streets—and not solely on the merits of the Round Tent, which was months away from being packed up and sold. Whimsical monikers like the Elephant House, Mansion House and Empire would soon roll off the tongues of giddy Argonauts. All three upstarts stood near shoulder to shoulder to the south of the Round Tent, on J and Front Streets. A passage from the May 28, 1893 *San Francisco Call* paints a vivid picture of Sacramento's Gold Rush saloon hub: "Gambling houses occupied prominent places on both sides of J Street and part of K, from the waterfront to Seventh Street and the sidewalk were encumbered with the tables of three card monte sharps and stands of other swindling games. From 12 o'clock in the day until past midnight the street gamblers plied their rascally arts along the thoroughfares."[88]

The Mansion House possessed rather chaste origins. Situated at the corner of Front and J, the building had been home to Sam Brannan's original mercantile, also considered by many to be the first framed structure in Sacramento. It should not surprise that Brannan, successful as a merchant and land speculator, grew into quite a gambler. So good was Brannan that he was known to have placed $10,000 in gold dust on a single hand and $18,000 on a single roll of roulette, winning both.[89] Additionally, his well-deserved reputation for enjoying wine and women is expressed in a *Salt Lake Daily Tribune* story from 1877: "Samuel was a sly old boy and lusted after fair maidens, matrons, or even widows of Zion." It goes on to say, "Samuel grew

Energetic "Jack Mormon" Samuel Brannan wasn't to be denied in his bid to make Sacramento a commercial hub. He also enjoyed drinking, gambling and rowdiness. *California State Library.*

fat in the land of Gomorrah and in the hours of his prosperity became filled in the spirit—not of the Holy Ghost, but the spirits of Bourbon."[90] While it is easy to acknowledge Brannan's being more than a business match for Sutter, how likely would it be that the city's two most prominent figures/ founders turned out to possess the loosest of morals?

However, in 1849, business came first for Brannan, who seldom hesitated to liquidate property, which he did with his riverfront store. By December of the same year, the Mansion House (née Brannan Mercantile) was in place. Its manager was Edwin Waller, a Texan who was in his late twenties. Waller's associates included barkeeper Michael Brannan from New York (no relation to Sam), also in his twenties, and elder barkeeper Joseph Reynolds, who was in his late fifties and from Missouri. The person of Edwin Waller is curious from a biographical standpoint. Based on census information from the states of California and Texas, it's probable that he was a major in the Second Texas Cavalry in 1861. Between 1862 and 1865, he rose to the rank of lieutenant colonel in the Thirteenth Texas Cavalry Battalion. In this capacity, he conducted partisan activities in southern and western Louisiana and eventually participated with Confederate units in the battles of Mansfield and Pleasant Hill.

In many ways, the Mansion House was a typical Gold Rush saloon. There were crazed dogs. Yes, "a dog, supposed to be mad" rushed into the House "foaming at the mouth and snapping at everything it could reach." After clearing the saloon, Waller picked up a Colt revolver and shot the dog. Save for the animal, no injuries were recorded.[91] There were gunfights. A few months later, the August 5, 1850 *Sacramento Transcript* would recount the deranged and drunken actions of a Brannan; in this case, John (no relation to either Sam or Michael). After being tossed two times from the saloon, the aggressor returned with gun in hand. Having been forewarned of Brannan's designs, the Mansion House's barkeep that night, a Mr. Winters, stood in wait with a firearm as well. When Brannan entered the saloon, the employee took aim and delivered a nonfatal shot into the "fleshy part" of the renegade miner's thigh, leaving him incapacitated and ready for arrest.[92]

Finally and perhaps most significantly, there were disputes over honest play. It was two o'clock in the afternoon in late February 1851. Although days from being outlawed, the practice of placing gaming tables upon the sidewalks outside their businesses was still embraced by owners. Seated at one table was Frederick J. Roe a young Englishman, gambler and dealer.

French monte was the game, one that maintained a dubious reputation for being easy to fix. Accordingly, one of the spectators, a miner, was suspicious of play and brazen enough to say so. In response, the intoxicated Roe recoiled with what equated to "play or go."[93] After the miner instructed Roe to "go to hell," a fistfight erupted, one that Roe and three allies were winning with a huge crowd watching.[94] Charles Myers, a local wheelwright from Columbus, Ohio, who could not "stand and see such things going on, without lending

G.V. Cooper's 1849 lithograph of Sacramento's J and Front Street hub shows the Mansion House (T) and Empire (S) and Gondola (Q) saloons. *Library of Congress.*

[his] assistance," intervened, throwing Roe to the ground and exclaiming, "For God's sake…if you want to fight, now have a fair fight and don't three or four of you jump on the poor devil and kill him in the street because he has no friends."[95] Seconds later, Roe jumped to his feet and, hunched over, searched the crowd for Myers. After spotting him, Roe snarled, "There is the damned son of a bitch that held me."[96] Roe then pulled a gun, steadied himself and aimed it toward Myers's head. In response, the wheelwright fled toward the Mansion House for safety, but to no avail. Roe pulled the trigger.

After the ball entered Myers's head "just in front of the left ear and passed into the lower part of the brain," his limp, soon-to-be lifeless body fell to the dusty ground.[97] Observers recount, at this point, an atmosphere of shocked silence. The ostensible peacemaker, described by the *Transcript* as a "quiet and most respectable citizen," had been struck down both violently and suddenly.[98] Rolls in the dust, fisticuffs and other forms of generally innocuous violence were common during the early Gold Rush, but Roe's actions were not just mortifying to those who saw them—they were astonishingly new.

What a dramatic moment it must have been. Myers's body was lifted into the air and carried down Front Street and then up K Street to the blacksmith shop of a former partner of the wheelwright's, Joseph Praeder, a thirty-three-year-old Pennsylvanian. Upon arrival, Myers's body was examined and his wounds determined mortal. The likely examiner was thirty-two-year-old J.M. MacKenzie, city councilman, physician and fellow Ohio native. After hopping atop a wagon and decrying the deplorable state of affairs in which "citizens were shot down in daylight," MacKenzie went on to demand an investigation and strong punishment. The words quickly fomented the crowd into a frenzied mob that demanded nothing short of a lynching.[99]

With word spreading throughout the central city, other crowds were born, all drifting toward Roe's holding place, the police station on the corner of Second and J Streets. A number of attempts were made to quell the masses, including one by City Marshal N.C. Cunningham, who committed himself to letting justice take its course. It appears to have been at this moment that those in favor of informal justice formed their own committee. Distinguishing himself as the marshal's moral opposite—at least for a short period of time—was Dr. Gustavus Taylor, who, after examining Roe and ostensibly vouching for his safety, faced the crowd and helped seal the prisoner's fate: "Half an hour—if a decision is not made in that time I will head the crowd and take the prisoner out. A peaceable man has been shot down. If those who are now guarding the prisoner meant to shed blood, let it be so. The people are supreme and will be so now."[100]

It is not known whether Roe ever scoffed at Taylor's presence, but something had indeed affected the latter's attitude, very likely Roe's intoxication. Regardless, Taylor was pivotal in swaying the mob, now numbering some two thousand. With minutes passing, Taylor again chose to speak. The *Transcript* reported, "Taylor called on every citizen to arm himself. If the officers of the law thought proper to interfere and seek to protect the prisoner, when the jury had decided on the case, then said Dr. T., let the streets of Sacramento be again deluged with the blood of her citizens. Dr. T. was ready to sacrifice his own life, if necessary, to carry out the ends of justice."[101]

While Taylor ratcheted up the crowd's ire, the committee that represented the mob tried to conduct a somewhat formalized review of the facts. At this point, a bizarre twist took place: Roe was sobering up. This, combined with the arguments of those admonishing formalized, legal action, started to sway Taylor, who then asked the mob to reconsider. The crowd, now nearing five thousand, would have no part of it. Taylor was out, and moments later,

English gambler Frederick Roe was likely hanged from one of the tall oaks in the pictured Horse Market. *Sacramento Public Library.*

with the mob hitting critical mass, a large wooden awning was torn down and used as a battering ram. Soon after, the jail was breached and Roe taken to Sixth Street, between K and L, an area known for its patch of tall oaks. It was 9:30 in the evening, and Roe's benediction was contrite. He blamed "sudden impulse" for his actions and then, after drinking a glass of water, pleaded that "God have mercy on [his] soul."[102] Nearly eight hours after pulling a trigger at the Mansion House, young Frederick Roe was hanging from an oak tree. Making a strange tale even stranger is the fact that Myers did not pass until Roe was dead.

The Myers murder and Roe lynching occurred at a time when violence in Sacramento was on the rise. Shootings, robberies and muggings were all surging, and the citizenry's collective angst grew in kind. A sampling of this rising concern comes from the January 14, 1851 *Transcript:* "Within the last two months, there has been a fearful increase of crime throughout the entire length and breadth of our state. It is with difficulty, at times, that the inhabitants of our cities and larger towns are restrained from returning to that prompt and efficacious mode of suppressing crime, known as the Lynch law."[103]

In this regard, the significance of Roe's crime is remarkable. It was a watershed of sorts, where Sacramentans' morality and perceived concept of community would be put to a very severe test. Would formal justice be given a chance to sort through events and satisfy the community it served, or would the caprices of vigilantism and mob rule win out? In this case, the absence of any meaningful trust in the government's ability to solve problems meant that those who knew better, or felt they did, wrested control. The *Transcript* describes the vigilante committee as consisting of "some of the most prominent and respectable men in the city."[104] It was also composed, overwhelmingly, of merchants (nine of the fourteen) whose interests were elementary: safe streets brought patrons, and patrons meant profit.

For the common citizenry, the incident symbolized something other than good business. With the affair occurring nearly a year after the city's incorporation and with a legal system indeed in place, it was clear that the public's acceptance of organized rule needed considerable seasoning, a state not unique to Sacramento. A brief scan of the *Union* in days following the Myers murder reveals numerous lynching-related headlines: "Lynching Again," "Tragic Affair in Napa City—Murder and Probable Lynching" and "Another Man Hung!"[105] As statistics bear out, early Californians neither trusted existing legal institutions to be effective nor considered the repercussions of their own illegal actions. Between 1849 and 1853, the state experienced just over two hundred lynchings, whereas just a few years later, between 1859 and 1863, lynchings dropped to just under twenty.[106] Historian David Johnson offers the following interpretation of such figures: "The legitimacy enjoyed by these popular tribunals stemmed from the moral authority that Californians, like other Americans of their era, gave to the 'people' over the coercive power of the state." He continues by stating that the contemporary perceptions of ad hoc justice were "not described as the rage of an individual, but as that of the people taken as a single sovereign and in this respect rage and excitement served as an unerring sign that society's moral sensibility had been violated. Such outrage spoke to an inherent, natural understanding of justice, unreachable through the procedures of due process."[107]

The role of the Mansion House in the tragedy is also worthy of discussion. If it's true that Roe's repentance came after sobering up, the responsibility of the saloon as the germ of his murderous malaise is clear. Moreover, his drunken state and later change of heart certainly affected Taylor's moral compass; it is then feasible, based on this and certainly to those from the temperance camp, that Roe would not have murdered Myers without the aid of spirits. A curious notion in this regard is the absence of any temperance-minded comment regarding the event. Roe was drunk at the time of the killing; various citizens attested to this. Yet why did the anti-alcohol elements of the city not convert the incident into even the smallest degree of moral leverage? While we don't know for sure, it is likely that saloons simply proved too strong a presence in the city's political, social and economic life for the area's diminutive guard of teetotalers to make any impact. In other words, political clout soundly trumped moral clout in an environment where the saloon was responsible for so much that kept a city both smiling and solvent.

One of the Mansion's immediate neighbors was the Empire, described by one observer as "an immense room filled with gamblers and revelers."[108] Horace Bell, a visitor to Sacramento City during the summer of 1850, recalled a stroll down J Street as revealing "at every block…gambling houses in full blast, but all of inferior note, until you reached the Empire."[109] The saloon was located at 104 J, and compared to its immediate neighbors, it was tamer and even a bit more upscale. The fullest description of the Empire's size and décor comes from the June 26, 1850 *Transcript*:

> *The Empire Saloon is 75 feet by 55, giving an area to the floor of 4,125 feet. Both rooms present a magnificent appearance when lighted. Almost the entire front of the Empire consists of heavy doors, which being thrown open give to the room an elegant and inviting aspect. In the rear is a fine dining saloon, under the direction of Mr. Jackson.*
>
> *This establishment is kept after the manner of the first hotels of the States and it is certainly creditable to all concerned. Back of the dining room is a room elegantly furnished with mirrors, lounges, etc. The room is intended for private parties.*
>
> *The Empire Saloon certainly bear[s] the palm all the other establishments in the city.*[110]

Albeit so close to what symbolized Sacramento's grittier side in the Mansion, the Empire would be both more spacious and more elegant. Its dining area and private room meant that the Empire's business objectives were to be more diversified than its neighbors. According to the 1850 census, it maintained a large staff, including six waiters and four barkeepers.[111] The Empire also delivered top-flight entertainment, with its biggest headliner being the Tyrolese Singers. As indicated by their title, the quartet, consisting of two men and two women, came from Tyrol, a section of central Europe bracketed by Switzerland, Austria and Italy. A most flowery description of their debut, coinciding with the opening night of the Empire itself, tells us that "there was a perfect jam to hear the Tyrolese Singers, whose fame had preceded them…Dressed in a costume from their own clime, they attracted great attention; and when they concluded their first song, there was a strong manifestation for a continuance. Each of the singers wears a hat of the sugar loaf order, decked with ribbons."[112]

At this time, groups of various talent levels adorned many of the city's saloons within which "full bands, or choice musicians are engaged, whose discourse music the evening long."[113] The Empire maintained one of the best. One September 1850 newspaper review called the Empire's musicians "a crack band, whose music is worth going to hear."[114] Illinois physician Israel Shipman Pelton Lord invokes the Empire's power of musical persuasion with a lively description of "a brass band from their high 'vantage' ground, a balcony at one end, inciting them to madness."[115]

The obvious value of music within the saloon milieu segues us toward its strange absence between late August and late September 1850. A comprehensive search of public and private records reveals little insight into the oddity. It was announced in the August 29 *Transcript* that "the musicians of the city, whose sweet strains were heard in almost every saloon, have been allowed to retire, or in other words, music has been dispensed with by proprietors of the saloons. The blowers of trumpets, agile-fingered pianists and scientific 'fiddlers' were on a regular 'fiddle-dee-dum' on Tuesday night and the streets resounded with music from the grave to be funny."[116]

A possible clue may reside in the collective cacophony of so many saloons creating noise. An account from German novelist and traveler Friedrich Gerstäcker speaks to his experiences as a trained musician who, when arriving in Sacramento, was told by "American" saloon owners that all they wanted was noise. Gerstäcker continues, "And as these hells in some streets stood house by house, or rather tent by tent, the reader may judge what a deafening mass of sounds continually floated through the air."[117] Yet weeks later, and most relevant to the quality of talent at the Empire, readers of the *Transcript* were greeted with the news that "the advent of music once more in our Saloons seems to give general satisfaction. The splendid band that formerly played at the Empire have resumed their places and discourse their rich and accurately played pieces daily to hundreds of listeners."[118]

The musical moratorium corresponds to no other event. The cholera epidemic was two to three weeks off from the recommencement of tunes, while neither fire nor flood seem to have been factors. A clue to understanding

Again, G.V. Cooper's 1849 effort shows us the Front Street destinations of the Elephant House and the El Dorado Exchange. *Library of Congress.*

the nature of the ban, also found in the *Transcript* and in a blurb about the Oregon saloon, refers to the absence of music as an "experiment."[119]

Another notable stop for the Sacramento Argonaut was the Elephant House, which sat on Front between J and K Streets, just a few doors down from the Mansion House. If the miner were to speak of his participation in the Gold Rush, it was common to claim to have "seen the Elephant." Painted on the false façade of the saloon was an elephant with the words "the" and "house" placed to each side, making itself easily visible from any ship anchored along the embarcadero. In addition to its saloon-style offerings, the House, with a front of 40 feet in length by 150 feet in depth, provided lodging with "three tiers of bunks on each side" of the house.[120] Tenants paid a fee of $2.00 a night without food and fifty cents for a drink or cigar.

Adding to this original core, other saloons would establish strong names for themselves in this post–Round Tent era. Moving down J Street, one would encounter, in no particular order, the Oregon, Lee's Exchange, the Magnolia, the Woodcock, the El Dorado, the Humboldt and the Orleans House. The Orleans, located on Second Street, between J and K, was the first of its kind for Sacramento: a riverside palace that offered a saloon and overnight accommodations, as well as billiards and a reading room. From the outside, the Orleans's appearance was anything but subtle. Its multiple stories, handcrafted terrace overlooking Second Street and imposing façade made it one of the most impressive buildings in Sacramento and certainly the class of the city's hotel/saloon community. With that said, who could have known that the wooden Orleans was prefabricated, brought "around the horn" from New Orleans and built for $100,000?

In its initial phase, the Orleans's saloon opened on a Saturday evening in late March 1850. The *Transcript* describes the Orleans as "larger, more decorated and striking" than its rival, the El Dorado, which opened its doors concurrently to the Orleans. The Orleans's walls were viewed to be "rich and adorned with splendid paper hangings" with one "continental picture, heavy with ornament." Also adjoining the Orleans were "two splendid rooms…one containing several billiard tables and the other furnish[ing] an admirable retreat for gentlemen; newspapers, dominoes, checkers and backgammon can be found there, with which to while away the time."[121] While the Orleans's first floor was occupied almost entirely by its saloon, the private rooms of the Orleans, which opened in mid-April, were located on its second floor and possessed the same style concept as the lower floor. Further detail on the Orleans's spacious décor comes from a letter to the *San Francisco Courier* written by a recent visitor to the establishment, describing it as a building with "seventy-five rooms, capable of lodging one hundred and fifty persons. The tables in the dining saloon are extensive enough to admit two hundred persons at one meal."[122]

Another interesting description of the Orleans comes from Lord, who, in October 1850, referred to the Orleans as having "an immense saloon in front and two very large rooms in back; one with three billiards tables and the other a sitting room, furnished with dominoes, chequer [*sic*] boards, chess men, etc. The walls of the saloon are covered with paper, exhibiting modern Grecian scenery, in connection with the Turkish War, South American, etc., really splendid. And here the gamblers most do congregate."[123]

The Orleans's deluxe accommodations were a far cry from those of Sacramento's earliest saloons, which maintained the modest objective of simply making sure patrons could drink, gamble, smoke and be entertained within four walls, a ceiling and a floor. This earlier breed also catered to the scattered miner/laborer who, after a night out, would settle for the most basic of sleeping conditions, perhaps a bar top or a bedroll outdoors. By appearance alone, the Orleans sought to attract the higher strata of society, those living in the city as well as those passing through (e.g. politicians, merchants, professional gamblers). It also wielded a reputation for being "a favorite stopping place for celebrities of the day," including starlet Lola Montez, about whom we will speak of later.[124] In time, the Orleans became well placed within the nexus of Sacramento's political, intellectual and financial aristocracy. This area of Second Street between J and K Streets would come to be called home by Wells Fargo and Company, the chambers of the State Supreme Court and the *Sacramento Union*. Also by this time, the hotel had ascended to the position of depot for Wells Fargo stage transport.

While an archetype of the glamorous, multipurpose saloon, the Orleans also holds the distinction of having been a frequent meeting place for both political and nonpolitical groups and causes. Formal governmental meetings to discuss amending the city charter, developing firefighting companies and building cisterns to more easily fight fires were all held at the Orleans. Local Democrats also met there in late April 1851, nominating party members for city positions. Perhaps the Orleans's greatest moment came in February 1854, when the hotel welcomed local authorities to officially greet Governor John Bigler, state officers and members of the legislature with open arms. Sacramento was now the capital of California, with the Orleans House standing as the very first place of formal assembly for state officials within the river city.

Refined as it was, the Orleans entertained its share of shootouts and other affrays. One gentleman lost the "end of his nose" as a result of an airborne tumbler. Another row took place on November 3, 1852, between Roy Beam and Edward Eastbrooks. It rose from politics and deteriorated from there. When the smoke cleared, a Colt revolver had fired "four or five" shots, none of which found their mark, and according to the *Union*, "both parties were arrested and bound over."[125]

In proximity to the Orleans was Lee's Exchange, located at 46 J Street. It was the creation of Barton Lee, an early Sacramento real estate mogul, and built primarily as a saloon in early summer of 1850. It soon came to boast, much in the mold of the "concert saloon," Lee's Theatre Hall, a showcase for various forms of live entertainment. Despite one source accusing the Exchange's band of turning out "barbarous" music, it formed a viable trump to the Empire's musical prowess.[126] Opening just months after the saloon, the "splendid Concert Room" on the Exchange's second floor was reported to be "well ventilated and capable of seating twelve hundred people," a notable figure when one considers that when full, the hall held nearly one-tenth of the city's population.[127] The hall was mostly constructed of brick, with rough dimensions of 60 feet by 120 feet. Popular acts to grace its stage included the New World Serenaders, the Sable Harmonists, the New York Serenaders, the Acrobat Brothers, the Ethiopian Serenaders and the Tyrolese Singers. A performance at the Exchange typically cost from two to five dollars per person.

Lord's initial description of the Exchange's "great saloon below the theatre" reveals a spot "finished up in a style that would astonish anything coming from beyond the Rocky Mountains." The size of the saloon was notable, resting with dimensions of "100 feet by 75 and giving the superficial contents of 4,000 feet."[128] We also know that, at any given time, the Exchange could host as many as four hundred people who were "not at all in each other's way."[129] Further description of the Exchange comes from Lord:

> *It is fitted up like a palace and has a dozen or more tables of all kinds of "games." On one side is a counter, 30 feet long, behind which stands three fine looking young men dealing out death in the most inviting vehicles—sweet and sour and bitter and hot and cold and cool and raw and mixed.*
>
> *Again—elevated above the mass site a band of musicians playing—ever playing for the amusement of the spectators and gamblers and to attract the passers by.*
>
> *Occasionally a good song is sung. The walls are covered with pictures, many of them, men and women, almost or quite in a nude state. Everything is got up, arranged and conducted with a view to add to the mad excitement of gambling.*[130]

Lord also mentions the wages of the Exchange's gambling staff as being anywhere between seven and twelve dollars daily, plus board for their efforts.

Another account of the Exchange is a great deal less glowing. The *Call* described it as a "large gambling-hall of unsavory repute, where for a time swindling games of every description were in progress and where fights were of hourly occurrence." The paper goes on to call it "the principal rendezvous of the three card, cup-and-ball and dice sharks. The liquors dispensed were vile and at night the hall was a pandemonium; but the air of lawlessness pervading the place was attractive to the reckless and half-drunken miner."[131]

One of the more notable moments in the history of Lee's Exchange occurred in June 1850, just days after the saloon's opening, when Sam Brannan (yes, that Sam Brannan) and a group of friends entered the saloon to drink. Prior to their visit, Brannan had been seen pushing a comrade through city streets on a wheelbarrow while simultaneously beating a

"Chinese gong."[132] After a lengthy period at the Exchange and "a little before daylight," Brannan and his colleagues carried their revelry onto the Levee, where they—crowbars in hand—mounted an attack on a squatter's hut.[133] For their actions, Brannan and his retinue were found guilty, but the penalty—a fine of $200—proved a pittance for the affluent rabble-rouser.

A more amusing tale from the Exchange originated from an incident that took place in February 1851 and involved H.C. Norris and Louis Leclare.[134] Over an unknown issue, Norris pulled a knife and Leclare a gun. However, just as the latter planned to fire, the ball rolled out of the pistol's cylinder and fell to the ground. It is not known what happened after that, but the affray soon ended with Leclare departing (one can assume quickly) for the Crescent City Hotel, where he then ate supper. While there, Leclare received a challenge from Norris to duel that afternoon at three o'clock, which he accepted. However, even at this early stage in California's legal development, dueling was an illegal activity, and the two were arrested.

The duel was a somewhat common fixture in early California's saloon circles. Despite its illegality (as strictly outlined in the state constitution), everyone from politicians to miners often invoked the *code duello*. Historian William Secrest attributes the marked presence of dueling in California to the large number of southerners who chose to participate in the Gold Rush.[135] Just as Europeans brought their beer, those from the American South imported their own cultural norms. In fact, more fatal duels took place between 1850 and 1860 in California than in any other part of the Union. Local churches attempted to discourage dueling by incorporating the topic into their sermons. The Reverend

Baptist minister O.C. Wheeler came to Sacramento in 1852, only to find himself preaching against dueling and drinking. *Sacramento Public Library.*

Osgood Church Wheeler spoke to a full house at the Baptist Church, located at the corner of Seventh and L, in early August 1852. The monologue amounted to an appeal for law enforcement officials to act more aggressively to enforce the anti-dueling laws already existing: "The laws we have are good enough and strong enough, if faithfully executed, to stop the evil in a single day. But laws unenforced are not only a shame and a disgrace; they are a decided curse to any people."[136]

While on the topic of cultural import, it bears mention that, for a time, Lee's Exchange also was a venue for prizefighting. Born in the British Isles, bare-fisted sparring made its way into America in the early 1800s. Its function as a male testing ground meshed well with Sacramento's Gold Rush demographics. As early as June 1850, the *Transcript* describes "Yankee Sullivan and his gentlemen" giving "displays of pugilistic skill" and states that "Mr. Sullivaa [*sic*] will be happy to put on the gloves with any gentleman who may request it. A fine opportunity is now offered to all who desire it, of seeing this celebrated pugilist while displaying the excellencies of his art."[137] One match, pitting Sullivan against a man called Van Arnam, was set for 8:00 p.m. on June 19, 1850, at the Exchange. Although details are scarce, we do know that Sullivan won the bout.

Sullivan's story is an interesting one. Born an Irishman in 1813 with the given name James Ambrose, he moved to England during his late teens. While in London, he boxed, robbed and murdered his way into a trip to prison at Botany Bay, Australia. After serving time, Sullivan stowed away on a ship, eventually making his way back to England. Once there, Sullivan got lucky: he fought and beat one of the better boxers in the country. With such prestige in tow, Sullivan made his way to New York City, where his sparring career took flight in earnest. Beating several notables along the way, Sullivan opened his own boxing academy in Brooklyn in 1842. This, however, was far too normal a lot for the Yankee, who soon drifted back into crime by fixing various fights and involving himself in the first sparring fatality in the country. In the aftermath, Sullivan fled west, where he fought in San Francisco and throughout the Mother Lode. He even made his way back to Sacramento to fight again, in both 1854 and 1855, at Holmes's Saloon on Second Street. His undoing came a few years later when he fixed various local elections taking place in San Francisco. After being found out by a San Francisco Vigilance Committee, he was thrown in jail. Having lived an interesting yet dysfunctional forty-three years, Sullivan was found dead in his cell on April 1, 1856. His demise was likely due to a severe cut on his arm that caused him to bleed to death.

Incorrigible and well-traveled Irishman Yankee Sullivan was one of Sacramento's earliest boxing attractions and a nationwide political strong arm. *Sacramento Public Library.*

Although most of the early stage performances at the Exchange were musical in nature, live theater appeared after its 1851 purchase by Doctor Volney Spalding. After his management of the city's first hospital resulted in an official investigation and consequential removal from his post, Spalding needed something new. The Harvard graduate's interest in both theater and real estate led him to purchase Lee's Exchange. This resulted in an overhaul of the venue and an immediate disbanding of the saloon. Despite Spalding's chief hope to transform the Exchange into a theatrical hub, he soon recognized—and wisely so—the obvious allure of maintaining a saloon. The result was the establishment of the American Saloons, which were located inside the theater. It is not entirely clear how many saloons there were, nor is it known if they operated independently from the theater, but patrons could expect "the choicest liquors and the most fragrant cigars...kept constantly on hand."[138]

Finally, it is worth noting the few degrees separating Lee's Exchange from John Wilkes Booth's assassination of Abraham Lincoln. The assassin's brother, Junius Brutus Jr., was the first manager of the American Theater, and all the Booths, save John, would come to play Sacramento: Junius Jr. in *Othello* and *Richard III*, Junius Sr. in the *Iron Chest* and Edwin in a number of roles. The family held a varying presence in the Sacramento acting scene for years to come, ending with Edwin, like brother Junius years earlier, playing roles in *Othello* and *Richard III* in 1887.

The most natural sobriquet for the Gold Rush saloon had to be the El Dorado. The best known of the El Dorado bloodline was brought to life for $26,000, in late October 1850, at the northeast corner of Second and J Streets.

Founded by Reuben Raynes and Samuel P. May, the saloon was described in the *Transcript* as being "simple, chaste and beautiful" with high, white walls and elements that conjured "a simple chasteness and classic finish to the room." The paper goes on to describe walls "ornamented with a few simple oil paintings, colored engravings and with elegant mirrors."[139] In overall appearance, an eyewitness described the El Dorado as a "large saloon in the great brick building… beat[ing] everything in the city, except one," that being the Orleans.[140]

Acting savant and Unionist Edwin Booth spent considerable time in Sacramento, acting at Lee's Exchange and other spots. *Center for Sacramento History.*

Vouching the described detail is the only existing depiction of the interior of an early Sacramento saloon. It was presented in the June 5, 1852 *Illustrated London News* and shows the grand height of the El Dorado's ceilings with a series of ornate chandeliers, an elevated bandstand, tall windows with thick, flowing drapery and wall-to-wall people, most American and Anglo-European, some Mexican and some Asian and African American, but all gambling, gawking and/or drinking—much like our earlier description of the Round Tent. The *News* correspondent also described the El Dorado as a place

> *where thousands of dollars change hands daily. There are in this room twelve banks of gambling tables, each having from five to twenty dollars. The games played are monte, faro, roulette and dice bearing the six first letters of the alphabet. Nearly everyone has his Colt's revolver under his coat, secured by a belt. There are a pianist and violin players, who perform in the orchestra day and evening. Every colour, complexion and country of the universe may be seen grouped together here.*[141]

This 1852 lithograph shows the El Dorado Gambling Saloon and a rare interior view of a Sacramento saloon. *Sacramento Public Library*.

Years later, in 1893, San Francisco's *Call* brought further description to the El Dorado, calling it the "largest and most attractive gambling-house in Sacramento," boasting a "bar fifty or sixty feet in length extending down one side of it and ten or twelve gambling tables ranged along the opposite side." The paper further paints the bar as an "elaborate piece of workmanship…furnished with silver and cut glass and against the wall back of it hung mirrors worth a thousand or more dollars each and oil paintings of still greater value."[112] Suspended near the rear of the saloon on a platform were ten to twelve musicians. Two notables were violinist Professor Meyer and pianist George Pettinos, both of whom played together at the El Dorado in 1851. We also know that the upper floors held several private rooms, including spots for large-stake gaming. In the words of the *Call*, "no one with less than thousands to hazard was admitted to these games, where fifty-dollar slugs, double eagles and golden ounces were the coins usually applied in betting."[113]

In regard to El Dorado violence, Lord speaks to an incident, just prior to Christmas 1850, when "five or six men blazed away" at a gambler named Ross. His return volley "passed between three persons who had been standing at the bar and made a deep indention in the counter."[114] As bystanders started to flee, police corralled one of the aggressors and the others escaped. Gold Rush Sacramento's violent streak and community of saloons necessitated a police presence. One had been in effect since 1849, with the appointment of N.C. Cunningham as city marshal. His original force consisted of two deputies, which expanded to twenty full-time officers in 1852, with ten on duty at any given time. For an agency that was making an average of 145 arrests a month by 1853, patrolling the city must have been harrowing.[115] Thanks to the Common Council, salaries for both the chief of police and his deputies were raised considerably in the summer of 1852. However, still lagging in 1854 were police accommodations at the station house. Their substandard condition—perceived to be worse than that of the holding cells—coincided with a rash of officer illnesses "in consequence, it is thought, of the dampness of the brick floors and the excessive ventilation of the rooms."[116] Amid public and press sympathies, this aspect of the department appeared barely tolerable, even for their "unceasing…exertions to ferret out and bring to justice the many thieves in this city."[117]

One notable encounter between the police force and rowdies took place at the El Dorado in December 1851.[118] While on patrol, an Officer Chandler came upon a disorderly group led by one Charles Turnbull. After locating the rabble-rousers inside the saloon, Chandler and partner Officer Hayward approached with deliberation. But just as the party was told that an arrest was imminent, someone struck Hayward violently across the face with a pistol. When the dust cleared, the perpetrator, a man named Barnes, was apprehended, and the issue appeared to have passed. Further into the evening, however, the ringleader Turnbull was mysteriously shot while retiring to his room. He survived his wounds, but the burning question related to who committed the crime. Was it Chandler, avenging the brutalization of his colleague? Or perhaps it was Hayward, seeking vengeance for the same? Whatever the case, the facts are few, and the story has been lost to the fogs of history.

Just days later, an El Dorado shootout between gamblers Thomas Moore and Alexander McAllister illustrated the various perils awaiting the saloon manager. With there already being bad blood between the two, McAllister entered the saloon at about 10:00 p.m. looking for Moore. When McAllister found Moore, the latter was in conversation in the rear of the saloon with manager Raynes. After Moore exclaimed "Stand off, I want nothing to do with you," McAllister took his weapon and fired at Moore, but with no effect.[119] With Raynes lunging at the shooter, Moore then fired four shots at his foe, all of which connected. The *Union* described the first shot as "entering the scrotum, pass[ing] through the intestines and out the crest of the ileum."[150] This was the shot that, after thirty-five minutes of what must have been unthinkable pain, left McAllister dead. Raynes sustained a gunshot wound to the hand. Moore was immediately taken into custody by police officer Whittier and then tried in court, where he was found innocent under the judge's ruling of "justifiable homicide."

The El Dorado was also a venue for the deft skills of one of the region's true celebrities, gambling savant Charles Cora. An immigrant from Genoa, Italy, via New Orleans, Cora had the idea of prospecting not through hidden veins of ore, but by way of felt-topped faro tables. His one known El Dorado appearance culminated in an epic shootout with a different Thomas Moore on October 26, 1852. The spat grew "out of some previous dispute at the gaming table."[151] Affairs started inside the El Dorado but soon made their way onto J Street, where several shots were fired. With no injuries recorded, both men were arrested and held on $1,000 bail, but it is likely that the affluent Cora spent little time in jail.

Italian-born Charles Cora became a legendary gambler but was hanged in infamy in 1856 by the San Francisco Vigilance Committee. *California State Library.*

Not three later, Cora was again involved in a shooting, this time at the Challenge Saloon with a John Lenear. Bystander P.S. Schermerhorn, a laborer in his early forties from New York, was hit in the groin by a stray bullet. Cora's name will surface again later in our discussion.

On a much lighter note, it was the El Dorado that illustrated how saloon fighting was not the sole province of the customer. In December 1851, two of the saloon's musicians got into a scrape "as they were mounted up in the orchestra box exposed to full view of the crowds below." The *Union* continues to tell us that "the piano artist, although by far the larger man, was rather worsted in the conflict." In the end, it appears that both parties mended ways and "struck up and performed the next tune with uncommon spirit."[152]

As of March 1851, the Humboldt, resting at 28 J Street, was vying strongly with the El Dorado for crowds.[153] Perhaps the most colorful—albeit grim—Humboldt description comes from Horace Bell:

> *Imagine yourself at the Humboldt, away out on J Street—a grand rag palace or gambling hell, literally swarming with gamblers and desperadoes of all classes and nativity, with brazen-faced, gaudily-dressed, painted and powdered harlots, who sat beside the gamblers at the monte banks, faro tables, rouge et noir, lansquenet, roulette, rondo and other games; but I hereby bear witness that these games were played at the Humboldt with a greater degree of fairness, integrity and honor than could have been found in any other country on the face of the earth, because if a man was caught cheating he was killed on the spot.*[154]

On one day at the Humboldt, in September 1850, two different gamblers were nearly killed over gaming disputes. One of them was "dangerously stabbed in the head," while the other was "horribly disfigured in the face."[155] One month later, the saloon hosted an altercation between two men, Dunn and Russell, over the "ownership of $40." It resulted in Russell clobbering Dunn with a four-pound weight that cut "through his hat and inflicting a most dangerous wound on the back of his head."[156]

A classic Humboldt tale of long odds and born legend was relayed, also by Bell. At one end of the encounter stood twenty-year-old Joseph Stokes, a mild-mannered Sacramento bookkeeper and son of a Philadelphia banker. Typically a modest observer of gambling, Joe became so much more than that one evening at the Humboldt. At the end of the business day and with saloons going into full swing, Joe, like so many young men, wanted to be part of the action. While watching a game of monte, he grew suspicious of Tom Collins, a renowned gambler and, as Bell puts it, "first class fighter."[157] Tensions spiked when Joe accused the dapper gambler of "drawing waxed cards while dealing." After hearing the accusation—libel of the highest degree in the gambling community—Collins softly counseled Joe to leave the saloon, giving him two minutes to do so. Refusing, Joe calmly dared the gambler to dispatch of him. Collins jumped from his chair and pointed a gun at the bookkeeper's head. Joe's reply? "If you are cowardly enough to shoot an unarmed man then blaze away. I don't belong to the breed that runs." Immediately, three shots were discharged from Tom's gun. At a distance of ten feet, one round grazed Joe's head, a second missed and the third hit his upper arm. When a bystander provided Joe with a loaded revolver, he aimed and fired. Seconds later, the great Tom Collins lay dead on the floor of the Humboldt, with a bullet hole in his neck. It is not entirely clear where the brazen Joe went from there. However, Bell does give the reader the impression that he morphed into a kind of noble terror, roaming the West, intimidated by none and ever dedicated to ensuring a fair fight.

The Humboldt's run was short. A few months after the *Transcript* intimated the decline of gambling activity at both the Humboldt and Lee's Exchange the paper announced the sale of the Humboldt's furniture and fixtures in May 1851.[158] The residential vacuum was soon filled by a new saloon called the Oriental. The saloon debuted in July 1851 under the management of Samuel Colville, an Irishman in his mid-forties. The ambitious Colville came to California in 1849 on the steamer *Isthmus* and never looked back. He would also draw distinction by becoming the printer of several of Sacramento's annual city directories.

Early on, the Oriental was "fitted up in the most splendid and costly manner altogether with a view to the comfort of its patrons." It also boasted a cigar stand, under the capable hands of a "lady"; billiard tables; and four splendid bowling alleys.[159] Though such features were nice enough to attract many a patron, a common thread between saloons—both in Sacramento and nationwide—was a desire to lure customers through some great novelty. Any number of factors—auctions, lotteries, art, musical acts, theater and often the unexpected—all served as the veritable "hook." In the summer of 1851, the Oriental's "hook" was "a practical exemplification of the famous 'bloomer' dress."[160]

As the *Union* correctly states, Bloomerism was "a style of female dress lately adopted in Eastern cities, first introduced by Mrs. Bloomer and daughters."[161] Bloomerism, energetically promoted by one Amelia Bloomer, was a radical shift in women's fashion that advocated an external dress that was fitted just above the waist and hung down three or four inches below the knee. Fitted under the dress were flowery, frilly pants that fastened just below the ankle.

The trouser-like look elicited praise from those who promoted women's rights and a desire to live in something other than the traditional confines of the heavy, uncomfortable dress. In fact, suffrage icon Elizabeth Cady Stanton "was delighted with the new style and adopted it at once."[162] This fresh fashion ideal, symbolizing freedom and a shift in the image paradigm, quickly made its way to California, where it would stick, but only briefly. As

Bloomers were more than a fashion alternative; they were a way to get female-starved miners and laborers into Sacramento's Oriental Saloon. *Library of Congress.*

the impractical dictates of fashion wielded a greater power than the practical comfort of the Bloomer, the style found no permanence in California. Be that as it may, Colville's Oriental did its part to promote a newness that went far beyond a simple change in fashion and well into the realm of breaking the conventions of tradition. What's more, in an environment where chances to spy the female form came few and far between, a look at such revolutionary garb must have done the dusty miner's heart good. That said, like its predecessor, the Oriental didn't last long. In fact, by July 1852—not more than a year after opening—the Oriental was put up for sale.

A somewhat forgotten pastime of Gold Rush Sacramento was bowling, an ancient game brought to America by Manhattan's early Dutch settlers.[163] Once here, the sport's popularity grew and, with the coming of the nineteenth century, possessed a particularly strong hold with the immigrant-laden American working class. Accordingly, the construction of bowling alleys in saloons sealed what seemed a natural marriage and created what would be referred to as the "bowling saloon." The saloon was, in fact, where the sport was originally showcased to the masses, and although not as popular as gambling, it soon surfaced as a legitimate diversion for a large cross section of Americans, including Sacramento's Gold Rush community. The local *Union* expressed its excitement for bowling by not believing that there was a more healthful or rational exercise than rolling Ten Pins, while also extolling the erstwhile Oriental for hosting a place "congenial to persons wishing exercise alone."[164]

Mentions of Sacramento bowling can be traced back to Heinrich Lienhard's reference to Peter Slater's maintenance of an alley at Fort Sutter's central building. In the context of time, this was well over a year before much at all existed at Sutter's Embarcadero, let alone at a saloon. It was not until 1849 that the first bowling saloons made their way into Sacramento proper in the form of the Humboldt, the El Dorado Exchange (at Front and J Streets) and, soon thereafter, the Oregon. Even though details are scant, the Humboldt was described as containing lanes that were separated from the rest of the saloon by an oilcloth curtain. And as we know, its replacement, the Oriental, continued to run alleys even to the extent of holding tournaments, with winners receiving prizes in gold. Even less is known about the Oregon, which was described by Lord as running "three bad alleys,"[165] while the Cooper lithograph identifies the establishment as the "Oregon Bowling Saloon."

In all fairness, the Oregon, which opened in August 1850, was much more than what its bowling alleys could offer. Under the management of William L. Chrysup, a native of Kentucky, and L. McGowan, the Oregon fit the Sacramento saloon archetype, providing musical entertainment and boasting an elevated orchestral perch "at the upper end of the room."[166] The saloon also hosted a number of minstrel groups, singing "Ethiopian songs, with banjo, violin, tambourine and 'bones' accompaniment."[167] Renowned

California architect A.P. Petit executed the design and construction of the Oregon, which the *Transcript* declared a "splendid and new saloon." The paper went on to call the Oregon "one of the neatest saloons in the city" and commended its taste in art, particularly a copy of William Sidney Mount's *The Power of Music*.[168] The piece presents a young African American male who, with a smile on his face and standing out of sight outside a saloon door, listens to music being played by a hard-fiddling European American.

In this pre–Civil War era of racial compartmentalization, Mount's piece was precocious. Individuals may have been oppressed into understanding their proper social place, yet there were indeed ties that bound classes, sexes and races, with music certainly being one of them. Contrasting as much is a story relayed to us by de Rutte. He recalls enjoying a drink in the saloon of the Hotel de France when in walked a man of mixed European and African race. The owners, two French women, served the man and naturally took his money. In seeing this, the whites that were present, many of them politicians, recoiled. As de Rutte states, "At the sight of the [customer] swallowing his

Mount's *Power of Music* presented a dose of guarded optimism at what music could do for antebellum America's social climate. *Cleveland Museum of Art.*

drink, the senators and representatives stood up as one man. Refusing in their haughty indignation to accept change for their money from the same hand which had just served a negro, each of them silently placed a dollar on the bar. Then like a herd of frightened deer, the gentlemen disappeared out the door, never to return."[169]

What does this incident say about the racial climate of Sacramento in the early 1850s? Although it says a good deal, there is yet more to the story. It is undeniable that racial tensions, especially those engendered by Gold Rush jealousies, ran high. They were even institutionalized through state law when the 1850 Foreign Miners Tax was enacted to tax non-Americans a percentage of whatever they pulled out of the ground. The tax extracted twenty dollars per month per noncitizen for the "privilege" of working the mines. Although such behavior was patently xenophobic and racist, it is important to note that it was not entirely transferable to the saloon milieu.

From the international mobs at the Round Tent to lithographed visions of a diversified El Dorado clientele, Sacramento's saloon culture could enjoy, at least on the surface, interludes of general tolerance. What's more, and with some exceptions, African Americans, Mexicans, mixed-race South Americans and Asians could often use white-owned saloons with some degree of freedom, not to mention the nonwhites who were either employed or even known to possess their own saloons. Overall, a few factors seemed to have made Gold Rush California and saloon culture somewhat more tolerant than other parts of America. One reason may have involved the equalizing element of capitalism. Quite simply, saloons and other businesses wanted patrons. If that meant a moderation of one's previous views on race, then it seemed to have been done more often than not. One saloon in Marysville, known as the Round Tent, was more than willing to welcome its customers "with no regard to distinction of color."[170] Scottish physician and journalist John David Borthwick also speaks eloquently to this very practical form of democracy by stating that the "almighty dollar exerted a still more powerful influence than in the old states, for it overcame all preexisting false notions of dignity."[171]

David Johnson's "labor theory of value" has ample relevance in this regard.[172] Accordingly, skin tone appears to have mattered less in an environment where one's industry and guile often meant the difference between life and death. Likewise, it may hold true that when one is placed in a region where the most basic elements of humanity are of premium importance (e.g. intellect, industry and guile), superficial traits—color, ethnicity, nationality, accent and religion—quickly become less important.

That said, basic geography and the absence of exclusive institutions so common to the "civilized" eastern United States proved just as democratizing as Borthwick's observations of unbridled capitalism.

Also worth mentioning is California's status as a free state, meaning that slavery was outlawed in the state by virtue of the landmark Compromise of 1850, albeit at the heavy expense of the Fugitive Slave Act, which mandated the return of escaped slaves to their owners. What this meant for California was elementary: free African Americans could roam the state with at least some peace of mind that skin color had little legal bearing on their lives, a notion that appears to have transferred itself into many of the state's saloons.

A less influential, yet valid, factor relates to the great number of Europeans who were fleeing 1848's revolutions, the bulk of which started during the same month (January) that gold was discovered in California. English, Irish, French, German and Italian nationals were all subject to some level of political struggle, making the flight to the new American territory even more palatable with the news of gold. Based on their revolutionary principles, how likely is it that many of them would have belittled themselves to discriminate? Many lived as bourgeois liberals who, armed with education and the experience of life under divine-right monarchy, viewed the quality of a man to be intrinsically tied to his character.

France, the flashpoint of the revolutions, provided in one delivery alone and according to the *Union*, an influx of "two hundred representatives of 'la belle France,' many of whom immediately trudged mountainward with pipe in mouth, pack on back, casting care to the winds and as jolly as Frenchmen can be."[173] Just months earlier, another group of Frenchmen had quickly rushed out of Sacramento's Gem Saloon in an attempt to avenge the shooting of a countryman whose sole offense was advocating due process in the case of a Chilean man's possible murder of an American in the foothill town of Jackson. The Gallic presence in Sacramento became so profound that beginning in July 1853, a version of the *Democratic State Journal*, the *Journal Democratique de l'Etat*, was printed in French.

As the Gold Rush pressed on and foreigners streamed forth, Sacramento became increasingly quartered, with the greatest concentration of race-centered saloons settling within the city's westernmost wards. Notably, of the 962 African Americans who lived in California in 1850, most lived in Northern California and many in Sacramento, where they established corridors along both I and Third Streets. It is there that the city's 1854–55 city directory lists no fewer than twelve African American–owned business, including Albert Grubb's Delmonico Saloon (L Street between Third and

Fourth), Edward Hill and William Smith's St. Charles Saloon (Third Street between J and K) and Charles Taylor's Indian Chief Saloon (Third and I Streets). Overall, by 1860, Sacramento's African American population would come to make up 2.9 percent of the city's 13,785 residents.

I Street's Tennessee Exchange was a particularly popular refuge for African Americans. Although names and the exact location of the Exchange are unclear, clear enough is the area's violent side. One incident, between two African Americans, turned for the worse when the keeper of a gaming table, Augustus Ennen, was shot by an unnamed aggressor, all within the context of a "fascinating game of poker."[171] The dispute arose over the rightful ownership of a certain piece of property that was at stake in the game. The unidentified figure then took the money lying about the table and left. When challenged by Ennen, the stranger fired two shots, hitting the dealer in the stomach and wrist. For Ennen, the wounds were serious but not life threatening. The shooter escaped on horseback and avoided arrest.

The Gem, also on I Street and not to be confused with its J Street counterpart, represented the rougher-style saloon, much in the mold of the earlier Mansion House. One of its more notorious rows took place between African American William Green and Mexican Francisco Navares.[175] It was Independence Day 1852, and the hostilities rose from a game of monte. Navares, who was highly intoxicated, challenged Green, who in response pulled his revolver and fired three times. When all was done, Navares was mortally wounded and Green in custody of the police. After "intense suffering," the Mexican finally died on the following day. "By some quirk of the law," or so said the *Democratic Journal*, Green escaped hanging. Green's penchant for violence was again seen at the Gem in October 1853.[176] Over a game of cards, Green and a man referred to as "Negro Jim" pulled guns at one another, firing several shots in between. In the exchange, Green was hit, falling to the ground. After getting to his feet, Green fled but was eventually caught, as was the man who shot him.

Not all was so gruesome at the I Street saloons. The *Democratic Journal* relates the much more lighthearted story of a drunken African American fellow who, on an evening in early December 1853, just in front of the Tennessee Exchange, possessed "a bible in one hand and a psalm book in the other" and "imagined preaching to a Negro camp meeting." The sermon, however, turned out to be an abbreviated one because of "a weakness about the knees, precluding the possibility of standing erect without the aid of a pulpit to support himself upon."[177]

Not surprisingly, many nineteenth-century saloons were politicized. One such spot was the Magnolia, which, having opened in the spring of 1851 at 123 J Street, was described by the *Union* as "by far the most handsome and pleasing saloon in the city. There is no glaring splendor exhibited in its decorations, but a sober beauty pervades its appearance, as sober deportment characterizes its patrons. The floors are covered with the finest carpeting, the seats and sofas of high finish invite a lounge or a quiet rest. With the Woodcock on one hand and the Magnolia on the other, we can have no reasonable excuse for starving or thirsting."[178]

The Magnolia and *Union* appear to have enjoyed an amicable existence, despite the fact that the paper was operated by those partial to the Whig Party and the Magnolia's Kentucky-born owner, Benjamin Franklin "Baldy" Johnson, was a Democrat, a party referred to by the Whigs, most pejoratively, as "Locofocos." Johnson, however, was not the typical Locofoco in the eyes of area Whigs. In addition to his proprietorship, he was a city alderman and therefore influential. Looking as if both parties were intent on cultivating ties between one another, one passage in the June 1851 *Union* states that although a Democrat of the "darkest dye, [Johnson] is a most gentlemanly and polite host and of our citizens desirous of imbibing a cold cobbler or hot punch, will be certain of obtaining an excellent decoction at this Saloon."[179] The passage provides at least some view of the depth of interparty patronage at this time in Sacramento. Another newspaper entry—and harbinger of Sacramento's burgeoning political heritage—spoke to the ideological hothouse that Johnson's Magnolia had become by claiming "under its roof more politicians have been made and unmade than in any other five buildings in the state."[180]

The quid pro quo between Johnson and the *Union* seems to have ended in December 1851 with the saloon's sale to "Arnold & Barker." According to the same publication, Johnson and a co-owner decided to leave "for their former homes."[181] As an interesting aside, Johnson was known, during 1849 and the early months of 1850, to have kept the Magnolia's refreshments cool by refrigerating them in snow obtained from the nearby mountains. As stated in Thompson and West's history of Sacramento County, the "commodity"—acquired for thirty cents a pound—had to be "packed on mules a considerable distance before reaching the wagon road" and then into Sacramento.[182] The topic of refrigeration will be discussed further in later pages.

Across the city, business-to-business patronage between saloon and newspaper spanned the political spectrum. As evidenced by a few passages in

MAGNOLIA,

NO. 28 J STREET,

BETWEEN FRONT AND SECOND STREETS,

SACRAMENTO.

The proprietors having erected upon their old site, a capacious FIRE-PROOF BRICK BUILDING, embracing BILLIARD AND DRINKING SALOONS, SLEEPING CHAMBERS, &c., guarantee that for architectural elegance, style, character and comfort, it is not excelled by any similar establishment in California.

THE BILLIARD SALOON,

is furnished with Tables made expressly for this house, by the most popular makers in New York.

THE CHAMBERS,

are fitted up in the best style, with every accessory to comfort.

THE BAR,

being, as *in the old days*, under the immediate supervision of Mr. B. F. JOHNSON, insures that every thing pertaining to that department will be unexceptionable.

☞ House open at all hours.

B. F. JOHNSON & CO.,

Proprietors.

Kentuckian B.F. Johnson's Magnolia represented the most political (in this case, Democratic) that a saloon could be. *Sacramento Public Library.*

the *Union*, the staunchly Democratic Indian Queen on J Street, between Third and Fourth Streets, in spite of being a place of several partisan meetings, also had a tight relationship with the "enemy" newspaper. The saloon, operated by the tandem of the Daly brothers, James and Bernard of New York, and Jacob Remmel, supplied the *Union* with generous amounts of eggnog, thus earning mention in the paper. The Indian Queen was also fondly cited for its kindness in the *Union*'s competitor paper, the *State Democratic Journal*. The saloon's name, a clear reference to Algonquian maiden Pocahontas, was blended into this passage from January 1853: "Messrs. Daly and Remmel…know how to honor the name of the aboriginal princess by making the best of milk punches and dealing them out by the gallon, as the *Union* office can testify from a trial they had of its qualities on New Year's Eve."[183]

The platforms of Whig and Democratic Parties, the two most influential in this period of American history, were simple. The Whigs, a nineteenth-century spinoff of the National Republicans, favored the supremacy of Congress over the presidency and sought a program of modernization and economic development. The balance of their support came from the professional classes: bankers, storekeepers, factory owners and commercial farmers. On the other hand, Democrats, seasoned through the populist views of Thomas Jefferson and Andrew Jackson, favored a supreme executive branch. They also envisioned America to be a land where agricultural-based values were best suited for the development of a democracy. In their eyes, modernization would only create an elite class that would subvert democratic values. Immigrant groups, particularly Irish Catholics and Germans, plus those living in the nation's agrarian regions and the developing western states, typically voted Democrat.

By August 1853, the Whigs had established a "headquarters" of their own. Whig partisan Vincent Taylor seems to have been the catalyst for the spot that was located on Second Street. Known as the Whig Headquarters, it boasted a "large hall on the second story and a bar of the choicest spiritual manifestations, from which to derive strength and courage during the hot weather and strife of a political campaign."[184] One of the saloon's more notorious claims to fame and definite "hook" was its exhibition of the supposed head of Joaquin Murrieta—an area folk hero to some, but a scourge to others—and the hand of comrade "Three-Fingered Jack," a nickname for Manual Garcia. Both body parts were preserved in jars of alcohol. The *Union* provided particularly gruesome detail on the state of the head: "A protrusion of jet black hair falls below its ears, while the sightless orbs indicate them to have possessed at one time of a flashing luster, such as is

INDIAN QUEEN

The above well known SALOON, situated in the most central part of the City,

No. 78 J Street, between 3d and 4th Streets,

SACRAMENTO,

Has been furnished in the most costly manner, and still continues to be kept by the undersigned, who supervises every department personally, and who has spared neither pains nor expense in placing the

INDIAN QUEEN,

In rank with the very FIRST CLASS HOUSES of the kind in the country.

THE BAR,

As heretofore, will be found at all times supplied with the most choice

Liquors and Cigars,

Served up in the most proper manner. EVERY TASTE SUITED.

LUNCH

Is served up every day at 11 o'clock, A. M., and 9 o'clock, P. M.

Thankful for the very liberal patronage extended, he trusts by undivided attention to merit a continuance.

Attached to the SALOON, 2d Story, is a

BILLIARD ROOM,

Furnished with new tables, and retired from the Public thoroughfare.

JAMES DALEY,

PROPRIETOR,

78 J STREET, between 3d and 4th Streets,

SACRAMENTO.

The Daly brothers' Indian Queen grew to have multiple locations throughout the city, the first Sacramento saloon to do so. *Sacramento Public Library.*

common to a majority of the Spanish race and eminently so to that portion of it with craft, cunning or superior intellectual attainments."[185]

Another prime Whig watering hole was Radford's, operated by the interesting character of Captain John Radford. Located in the basement of Langley's Brick Building at 19 and 21 J Street, the saloon was described in December 1851 as "not quite completed," but "the furniture is costly and in excellent taste, while the spacious room will accommodate the patrons of the establishment."[186] The *Union* goes on to tell us that "the liquors, as well as everything else, were bought by Capt. Radford himself, which ensures them to be of unsurpassed quality."[187] The spot also endeavored to provide newspapers from all parts of the country, an effort not uncommon at many of the city's saloons.

Radford also seems to have had a reputation as an exceptional storyteller, not a bad draw for a new saloon. He spoke of the "excitements of a deer or antelope chase, the dangers of the bear fight, or the still more thrilling incidents of an Indian fight."[188] Radford was a devout Whig, therefore willing to host a number of party events, including a convention for the selection of candidates for the city's First Ward in the spring of 1852. The saloon also made an effort to provide oysters as part of its complement of wares. Their availability, increasingly common at this time, must have been a warming comfort to those from New England. Radford obtained his oysters from Oregon, and it was anticipated that in a year, his saloon could offer "an abundance of oysters of the largest size and quite equal to those enjoyed by our more favored Atlantic friends."[189] They were also said to have compared favorably to oysters from the Chesapeake Bay region of the Middle Atlantic States.

Not to be lost in the many functions of the Gold Rush saloon is the element of prostitution. One of Sacramento's best-known spots for prostitution was the Palace. Located on Second Street between I and J and in existence at least as far back as November 1850, the Palace possessed several of the traits defining the typical Sacramento saloon: it served alcohol, hosted gambling and provided the occasional room for let. With prostitution legal at this time, the Palace and other spots preyed on the needs of scores of 49ers. To gauge the demand for paid companionship, one need only look in local papers to find advertisements for "Gonorrhea Mixture" and "Red Drop," which were sure to cure syphilis "without mercury or any poison."[190] The Palace's proprietor and madam, Fanny Seymour (also known as Fanny Smith or Fanny Sweet), is clearly one of the more fascinating figures in this period of Sacramento history. The *Union*, in addition to commenting on "her Grecian beauty," described the young Louisiana native as *tall and graceful in her person, but deficient in the feminine delicacy usually characterizing that order of women, with a keen perception, quick motion and dignified carriage. Her complexion is fair, with ruddy glow of perfect health; her eye is of light gray, strongly marked and expressing in an eminent degree the possession of strong passions and implacable animosities.*

...in the earlier years of the State, her belt was garnished with a revolver and bowie knife, whose threatening aspect was believed to be of no idle or mere braggadocio import; and the result has proven that she knew how to use, as well as display such weapons.[191]

Fanny was also an irrepressible gambler. She loved faro and was known to drink and gamble her way into wagering hundreds of dollars at a time. Nonetheless, she was stoutly independent, owned her own business and, according to the *Union*, possessed a personal value of at least $50,000.[192]

The defining moment in Fanny's Sacramento tenure came in December 1852. It was a Monday evening at the Palace, and Albert Putnam, a stage driver, sought the affection of a woman. Reports indicate that Fanny had been drinking and was likely intoxicated when she insisted that Putnam purchase a bottle of wine, a customary and mandatory act for someone sitting in the Palace's "wine chair," as Putnam was. The concept of the chair, common in many a brothel, was based on a trade: to sit in the most comfortable chair in the brothel meant payment in the purchase of wine. Putnam, while sitting in the chair, refused to do so. Not leaving things at that, he told Fanny to, in essence, sober up, "uttering a threat if she did not."[193] Given her defiant disposition, Fanny's response was perhaps predictable. She left the room, grabbed a Colt revolver, returned and shot Putnam in the back.

After the shot and realizing the gravity of her act, Fanny ran onto Second Street and found a police officer. Soon after reporting her deed, she was taken into custody and held at the city's station house. Unlike the Roe incident two years prior, the marshal was ready for any mob vigilance, placing Fanny within the safer confines of a boat—likely the prison brig *La Grange*—until the crowd's ire subsided. While the resolution of the Fanny saga appeared elementary, a twist developed. Much of her fate would hinge on the presiding judge's decision to offer bail. It is not clear why such was tendered in the event of what appeared a clear case of murder. Perhaps it was Fanny's gender, her status as a respected businesswoman or the fact that she was the mother of several children. Whatever the case, she was released on bail in early January 1853. Notably, those who bankrolled her release were the familiar names of Reuben Raynes of the El Dorado and D.V.M. Henarie of the Orleans. Patronage, again, seemed to play its part in city and social affairs. How likely is it that the relationship between all three figures, one based on business and mutual benefit, was a factor in prompting her release? Or perhaps it was Henarie and Raynes's modest desire to see a friend removed from jail? Regardless, she was out, never again returning to Sacramento.

Perhaps the most entertaining saloon moniker at this time was the Bull's Head, owned and operated by Captain Edward "E.J." Feeney. The name's origin likely relates to the bovine skull that sat either just outside or inside the saloon. Setting it apart from other establishments we've discussed, the Bull's Head was not on J Street, but rather Fifth and K. In addition to its operation as a saloon, it served as a polling place, eatery and boardinghouse, with single meals costing fifty cents and a week's lodging ten dollars. The saloon boasted a barroom, dining room, bake oven, stoves, its own horse stable, several rooms (either for office or residential use), a rear balcony and, according to the *Union*, an artesian well, "the only one in Sacramento city, which contains an exhaustless supply of water and is convenient and indispensable in the case of fire."[194]

The Bull's Head was also one of the first Sacramento saloons to have offered the "free and easy," an attempt by smaller businesses to employ a scaled-back version of the "concert saloon." The *Transcript* quipped at the nature of the event, stating, "What's a 'Free and Easy?' Now we do not know what the performance is, but the name is certainly ominous."[195] Anything but ominous, the "free and easy" was typically cheap and quick and involved a magician, comedian/actor or crooner—anyone who could add value to the saloon experience.

The tavern's proximity to the Horse Market, located at the intersection of Sixth and K Streets, made it a prime meeting place for both teamsters and stockmen. The Market was *the* place for the purchase of four-legged transportation, boasting a large selection of saddles, harnesses and carriages. It also served as a place where miners, as they ascended the foothills, grabbed supplies. The area's distinguishing landmark was a massive oak tree, providing an oasis during the area's hot summers as well as ample coverage from winter and fall showers. It is also likely that this is the same tree that Frederick Roe was hanged from. The *Transcript*'s March 20, 1851 description of the spot is as follows: "For a good portion of the day, this is decidedly the liveliest portion of our city. Day after day the auctioneer's hammer descends at the last bid of some 'lucky hombre,' yet the business does not flag. We expect this trade to continue a permanent and relative one, as long as the wants, whims and habits of Californians are what they are."[196]

Not short on bodies or on spots for congregation, the Market also saw its fair share of political rallies and, of course, a steady stream of gambling. Both French monte and shell gaming were common at the Market. The best description of the Market as a gaming hotbed comes from the March 15, 1851 *Union*: "Let's not leave the market without another passing glance at a few of its different phrases…'the tray, the tray! I'll bet six ounces on the tray,' comes shrieking from 'a chap' about 12 to 15 years old and small of his age…'who takes the bet?'…'will you take the bet sir?'"[197]

As a result of its proximity to the Horse Market, the Bull's Head was able to enjoy a profitable run. However, it also grew a reputation for being a spot of common misfortune. The first bizarre event took place in April 1850. As several workmen were in the process of blasting a sycamore tree on the corner of Third and K Streets, Bull's Head barkeeper, Gilbert C. Briggs, stepped out of the saloon to take in both the spring day and distant pyrotechnics. When the explosives cracked, a large piece of timber flew toward the saloon, striking the "door post where Mr. Briggs was standing." The impact sent shards of wood at Briggs's forehead and "over the left eye, crush[ing] and mangl[ing] that part of the head in a shocking manner." Tragically, the trauma left the New York City native dead and his "young and beautiful wife" an early widow, all the result of a simple curiosity.[198]

Some months later, the odd case of an unnamed customer occurred within the Bull's Head. Details are few, but one Saturday evening, "a man, apparently in good health, laid down upon a seat" at the saloon. Not long after, it was discovered that he had died. It was never determined what directly killed the man, but a later medical examination "ascertained that the deceased was diseased in several vital parts so seriously as to make it appear strange that he had lived so long."[199] Capping the saloon's run of misfortune was the sudden, accidental death of owner E.J. Feeney in 1854.[200] He was a mere thirty-eight years old.

Albeit overshadowed by their bent for vice, several of Sacramento's Gold Rush saloons could also cook. One spot deserving mention is the Woodcock, located on 15 J Street. Its original managers were a Mr. Reed and Edwin Cushing, the latter in his mid-twenties from New Jersey. By all accounts, the saloon established a reputation as a top restaurant, especially if one sought turtle soup. The Woodcock also claimed to have on hand "every variety of fish, flesh and fowl which the country affords."[201]

The Woodcock's layout seems to have been quite like many saloons of the time, containing a bar section and "dining saloon," both of which, according to the *Union*, were "in point of comfort and elegance, unsurpassed by anything of the kind that we have seen in the country."[202] As a thriving business, and operating with so many desirable commodities about (i.e. money, gold and liquor), the Woodcock, and spots like it, were ripe for break-ins. The Woodcock was violated in June 1851 when the lock on the front door was pried open, resulting in the pilfering of "nearly all the silver spoons in the house, a number of table spoons, boxes of preserved meats, jars of preserved fruits and bottles of champagne."[203]

Perhaps the most craftily executed job took place in January 1851, when Lee's Exchange was burgled for between $7,000 and $8,000 in silver. The saloon's gold was kept in iron safes, but the silver was held in "a large wooden chest lined with zinc."[204] Crawling some one hundred feet between the ground and the floor of the Exchange, thieves were able to—over a day or two—orient themselves to the location of the chest, bore up through the floor and chest, and extract the booty without detection. In the aftermath, emptied oyster cans, bedding, bread and liquor were found under the foundation "not worth a song in comparison with the haul they made."

This chapter's end takes us to November 2, 1852. Various sources tell us that the winds swirling about the city that Tuesday night were quite strong, "blowing a gale from the north."[205] It would be years later that news writer Frank Leach recalled the evening of the second as a "black" and "windy" night.[206] From a child's perspective—Leach was six years old at the time of the event—the fire's impact was indelible: "I shall never forget the sight. The force of flames arising from blocks of burning buildings and red light reflected against the heavy clouds to me looked as if the world were on fire."[207] The "awful conflagration," as Morse called it, started in Madame Lano's millinery shop, near Fourth and J Streets, and "with the rapidity of the thought the devouring element shot forth its lurid fangs fastening upon the frail wooden tenements."[208] By the time the last ember had dimmed, a total of fifty-five city blocks lay in ruin, with damage estimates running anywhere from $5 million to $10 million.

The fiery destruction meted out on the city's saloons was extensive. Most of them, made of the most ideal combustibles, were easily swallowed by the confluence of fire, wind and fuel. Within the unfortunate group were the Orleans House (well over $100,000 in damages), the Magnolia ($10,000 in damages), the Woodcock ($20,000 in damages), the Diana ($8,000 in damages), Lee's Exchange and the American Theater ($20,000 in damages), the Humboldt ($12,000 in damages) and the El Dorado ($50,000 in damages).[209] Although early reports declared a mere six fatalities, the grim truth was that others were dead but just not found. The first post-fire issue

The fire of November 1852 destroyed nearly 70 percent of Sacramento proper, including several saloons. *Center for Sacramento History.*

of the *Union* declared that a barkeeper had been burned to death, with no one having "heard his name or where he kept."[210] On November 7, the body of a man was exhumed from the wreckage of the Orleans House, and "the remains were so much charred it was impossible to ascertain whose they were."[211] Another *Union* dispatch revealed that, even in the wake of such grand disaster, shootouts were prevalent as ever. Two gamblers—one named Dart, the other Haney—fired at one another amid the ruins of the El Dorado, with the latter dying.[212]

Chapter 4
THE TIPSY PHOENIX: 1853—56

A s 1852 ended, 70 percent of Sacramento had been razed by fire. In the aftermath, the city responded impressively: within thirty days, citizens had mustered the construction of 761 buildings. Not surprisingly, 65 of them were brick.[213] In fact, by 1855, workers had laid an amazing twelve million bricks. So prodigious had Sacramento's brick industry become that when it was time for the U.S. Army to start building coastal defenses on Alcatraz Island in 1857, it was the River City that provided the brick.[214]

Most aggressive in rehabilitating itself was the Orleans House, but not under the guidance of its original troika of managers. Joseph Curtis, the last of the three to maintain interest in the structure, sold out to Misters David V.M. Henarie and Moore in late January 1852. Doing its predecessors proud, by mid-November, the duo resolved to rehabilitate the Orleans in its original spot, but "entirely of brick."[215] By mid-December, the Orleans stood four stories high, and on New Year's Day 1853, the saloon portion of the building was ready to open its doors.

The Orleans was the first of the pre-fire family of saloons to open, and it did so at a time when the embattled city needed it most. If the fire weren't staggering enough, New Year rains flooded the city. The *California Alta*'s read of the weather was that "the complete penetration of businesses of every kind can hardly be realized by you. The streets combined with the rain drive everyone in-doors. By 3 PM yesterday not a team or dray could be seen on J Street or the levee—a thing never known before in the history of this place."[216]

In fact, for many, attending opening night at the Orleans House meant that one had to either go by boat or swim. Regardless, whether entering the saloon that night with soaked britches or dry ones, the experience must have been a grand one. The Orleans's architect, Charles H. Shaw, spared little. The saloon alone measured some eighty-six by fifty feet, while ceilings reached sixteen feet high. Its cornices were "finished in mastic and stucco of virgin whiteness and its walls adorned with scenic paper of the most gorgeous coloring."[217] A special attraction of the saloon was its illumination by "Enson's [*sic*] patent oil gas," invented and patented by Mr. Thomas Ensor of New York City.[218] A total of five chandeliers, each with special burners, would provide artificial light in the saloon, while the entire hotel contained sixty.[219] The bar also contained four huge mirrors, each covering a dimension of twenty-four feet high by three feet wide. On its exterior, the Second Street façade of the hotel was built to awe. Not only did the Orleans's front walk boast three gas-powered lampposts, but patrons were also met by the grandeur of seven glass doors. With the last nail driven, the Orleans had cost $176,000, but for what the *Union* tabbed the "most elegant saloon in the State."[220]

So prestigious had the phoenix-like Orleans become that it was able to draw some of the finest entertainment in the West. In March, crowds again braved inclement weather to see violinist and P.T. Barnum darling Miska Hauser. The Austrian-born virtuoso played to a packed house that included a *Union* reporter who wrote that sounds from Hauser's "faultless bow were distinctly heard, like angel whispers, in every part of the room."[221] Days earlier,

The post-fire Orleans was both a palace and cultural hub for the early city. Its saloon was also the site of premier entertainment. *Center for Sacramento History.*

Austrian violin virtuoso Miska Hauser saw the best that Lola Montez had to offer. *Look and Learn, Limited.*

the New Orleans Serenaders were greeted with "unbound applause" as they treated viewers to "a pleasing variety of negro melodies, wit and stupidity—combined with dances, conundrums, [and] instrumental solos."[222]

The post-fire Orleans also served as host to one of the more beloved performers of the Gold Rush era, Lola Montez. The Irish-born actor/crooner/dancer was known for her suggestive "Spider Dance," which, while in Sacramento in July 1853, was performed in tandem with the "Ole Dance." The latter movement, according to the *Union,* "happened to excite the merriment of one or two persons sitting in front of the stage." However, taking the behavior—or what Montez coined "stupid laughter" coming "from a few silly puppies"—as a sign of disrespect, she refused to continue, exclaiming, "If my dancing does not please the audience, I will retire from the stage."[223] She did just that, agreeing to finish only after a brief performance on violin by Hauser. Far from traumatized by the event, the next day, the waif-like Lola "skipped up" to the violinist, exclaiming, "Dear Hauser, last evening was worth more to me than $1,000. I was delightfully amused and I have added another to the list of my adventures.'"[224]

By this time, we see the entry of James Hardenbergh, whose co-management of the Orleans qualified him for the city's small fraternity of saloon-running, Democratic politicians, along with B.F. Johnson of the Magnolia, James Daly of the Indian Queen and Reuben Raynes of the El Dorado (Raynes sought the office of alderman in April 1853). Like the Magnolia, the Orleans proved a spot of true politicking. For politicians of all ideologies, the saloon was a prime watering hole. In spite of "its admirable ventilation, [it could not] cool the heated brow or resolve the momentous questions, 'Will I be nominated and if nominated, elected?'"[225] It was also a venue where political sentiment could easily morph into political violence. Under the headline "Soiree Pugilistique," the April 13, 1852 *Union* described a row in which "legislators, ex-legislators and lobby legislators participated." The entry continues, "The optic of one of the parties was wreathed in mourning," with "no other damage done."[226] And like its pre-fire ancestor, the saloon was known to host nomination ratification meetings, including one for the Whigs in April 1853, when the bar "was filled to its full capacity."[227]

An indicator of Sacramento's large Yankee presence and, again, the saloon's culinary flexibility, came when the Orleans hosted a Christmas 1853 "New England Dinner."[228] Held in the saloon, the dinner consisted of a mouthwatering array of items familiar to the Northeastern palate, including oyster soup, salmon chowder, boiled salmon, barbecued perch, clam chowder and lobster salad. This is a far cry from other holiday fare to be served at much less sophisticated establishments, one being Richard Lockett's Nonpariel Saloon on 68 K Street. On New Year's Eve 1854, the saloon served a beaver lunch, the meal's benefactor—"the largest beaver of the season"—weighing forty-seven and a half pounds.[229]

Lola Montez played nearly the entire American West but would never forget her time at the Orleans Hotel. *Center for Sacramento History.*

A notable change for the Orleans came in the summer of 1853 with the erection of a new wing, measuring some eighty-five by thirty feet. The addition—made entirely of brick and affixed to the north side of the building—was designed to host the hotel's billiard tables, which had been located in the increasingly cramped saloon. It was also in this new section that a "gentleman's private dining" area and "ladies' ordinary, with private entrance" would be included.[230] Concurrently, George B. Bidleman replaced Hardenbergh and Henarie as the Orleans's manager. The Count, as Bidleman preferred to be called, christened his newfound control of the Orleans with a hearty celebratory meal of turtle soup. The 150-pound tortoise was transported from Mazatlan and transformed into soup that Bidleman and a bevy of friends took "no small portion of."[231]

By mid-decade, most of the city's saloons possessed at least one billiards table. Like boxing, the game's primary exporter was England. Although the cost of a table and accoutrements made it primarily an aristocratic pastime in the first half of the century, the industrial revolution and consequentially lower production costs brought billiards to the American masses. Once introduced, the game's popularity quickly blossomed. The earliest record of billiard play can be established as far back as October 1849 at the aptly named Billiards Saloon, located on K Street between First and Second Streets. Its first advertisement in the *Placer Times* guaranteed an environment "where an hour can be disposed of very agreeably."[232] One of the more intriguing billiard locations was inside the city's Forest Theater. Opening in fall 1855, the theater offered a chance to enjoy a quick game of carom, sip a drink served up by proprietor Moses Flanegan, and then sit for a dramatization of Harriet Beecher Stowe's *Uncle Tom's Cabin*.

Sacramento's earliest saloons imported their billiards tables from the east. However, as the city grew, so too did outlets for local production. A.H. Bening's Sacramento Billiard Factory opened in 1855 with a location on K Street, between Fourth and Fifth Streets. In an effort to dissuade prospective buyers from opting for an imported table, Bening emphasized the value of a table made of local wood, stating that "the dry climate of this country seasons the wood better than any place in the world."[233] By 1858, Sacramento had three billiard-table manufacturers, collectively turning out seventy-five tables per annum, each at an average cost of $600 to $700.

With the Orleans's new roominess, management decided to install a fountain in July 1854. Placed in the center of the barroom, it measured ten feet in diameter. The water was passed through a pipe and forced five to six feet into the air. The hope was that it would add "very much to the comfort of all who may be in the room, by cooling the atmosphere therein."[234] Who knew that Bidleman would soon opt to stock the fountain with fish for the very purpose of angling? In July 1856, the fountain became home to another animal, a pelican that had been gifted to the Count. After promising "to take excellent care of the bird," he deposited it in the fountain, only to find that it had disappeared after being visited by the Count's many friends. When asked about the absence of the "aquatic pet," the Count replied "d—n pelican! He eats twenty pounds of fish a day, and fish cost twelve and a half cents a pound!"[235]

Orleans Hotel,

SECOND STREET, BETWEEN J AND K,
SACRAMENTO.

The above Hotel, occupying a space of 85 by 150 feet, in the most central part of the City, built of brick, and three stories high, offers INDUCEMENTS TO TRAVELERS not surpassed by any establishment in the city, and unequaled in the country.

The second and third stories of the building is set apart for

PARLOR, FAMILY ROOMS AND CHAMBERS,

Furnished in the most costly and comfortable manner, and attended by polite waiters.

THE GROUND FLOOR IS SET APART FOR

Dining Room, Reading Room, Billiard Room, and Saloon or Bar Room.

THE TABLE will be found at all times supplied with the choice of the market, served up under the inspection of competent stewards, in a manner that cannot fail to suit the most fastidious.

The **Reading Room** is supplied with all the Daily Papers of the State, and the latest European and Atlantic news.

The **BILLIARD SALOON** is furnished with Tables of the finest workmanship, and superintended by an experienced keeper.

THE BAR will be found at all times supplied with the most **CHOICE LIQUORS and CIGARS.**

This Hotel is also the DEPOT AND OFFICE of the CALIFORNIA STAGE COMPANY, and within one square of the STEAMBOAT LANDING, making it the very center of traveling intercourse.

The House is open at all hours, and passengers arriving by the Boats or Stages in the night, can be accommodated with rooms.

HARDENBERGH & CORSE, Proprietors.

J. R. HARDENBERGH.   M. D. CORSE.

The sophisticated Orleans Hotel, like so many saloons at the time, was a political hothouse. *Sacramento Public Library.*

Come September, it was time to renovate the hotel's saloon, addressing what the *Democratic Journal* referred to as an "unwieldy and we may say uncomfortable space."[236] Also added was a veranda that covered the entire length of the building, a new coat of paint and expanded accommodations to meet the needs of three hundred residents. Management also saw fit to upgrade the quality of the billiards section of the hotel, spending $7,000 to do so. Such changes were required to accommodate, as we know, the urbane tastes of the city's burgeoning community of politicians who were so often to "swarm" the Orleans, "the great depot for present and prospective office holders."[237]

Not to be outdone by the Orleans, the El Dorado's co-owner, Reuben Raynes, also set to rebuilding, this time on the northeast corner of Second and J Streets. Raynes's immediate goal was the construction of a one-story structure that, by the fall of the same year, would be expanded by two more levels. In the interim, however, Raynes, armed with "plenty of nerve and money," didn't miss a beat as he set up a faro game operation under a tent near the old location. Just days after opening, Raynes, while occupying the tent's lookout chair, was approached by an eager gambler who asked about a betting limit. Excited by the question, Raynes replied, "The limit in gold, whether in blue chips or $50 slugs piled straight up, is the top of the tent, and if you say so I'll have it pulled up five or six feet for your special accommodation."[238]

By March 1853, a fully reconstructed El Dorado was back to its irritable self as visitors were stabbing each other with penknives; by April, the saloon was also back to its customary air of ballistic violence, with one such bout taking place between two gamblers, a Mr. Taylor and Washington Montgomery, the latter a Kentuckian employed at the Diana.[239] When Taylor contended that Montgomery owed him $10, the latter struck the former in the mouth. At this, the bloodied Taylor left the saloon to grab a pistol. He returned to the saloon with not only a firearm but also his wife. Standing at the ready with his pistol cocked for firing, Montgomery was grabbed by Taylor's wife. In the ensuing struggle, Montgomery's gun went off, hitting Taylor in the hand and his wife in the thigh. Neither wound proved serious, but both men were eventually arrested. Then, in the summer of 1853, a roulette dealer at the saloon, identified by the *Union* as "Dan-Something-or-other," robbed his employer of $900, escaping on a "2 o'clock boat."[240] Raynes sent an officer after him on the steamboat *Orient*, but it is likely that the perpetrator was able to catch an Atlantic-bound steamer, thereby avoiding apprehension. Not long after Dan's exit, Mr. Peters, a faro table operator at the saloon, was robbed when he literally fell asleep on the job. When he awoke, $975 was gone. The *Union* went on to report that "three Spanish boys and a woman…[were] arrested on suspicion of abstracting the money."[211]

At this time, we also see the resurrection of the Magnolia, under the guidance of none other than the returning B.F. Johnson, who, according to the *Democratic Journal*, "sold out, visited his old home and returned to the land of his adoption with a rose fit to be transplanted in our lovely valley."[212] Why he returned is not known, but in doing so, Johnson accomplished a magical rehabilitation of the Magnolia, as it opened for business by November 11, 1852, roughly one week after the fire. Although a simple frame building in the early going, it proved more than functional for the saloon until a more permanent structure was built. The last night in the makeshift Magnolia was celebrated on August 7, both by Johnson and his new partner, Volney Spalding of American Theater fame. Just days before the adieu, John Sutter's personal army, the Sutter Rifles, came by the Magnolia for an hour of "conviviality."[213] The Rifles, which eventually became California's Company A, 184th Infantry Regiment of the National Guard, were formed in June 1852.

Made entirely of brick, the new Magnolia rested at 23 J Street, between Front and Second Streets and just next door to the offices of the *Union* at 21 J. Built to the tune of $20,000, the saloon's final dimensions were twenty-two feet in the front, with a depth of ninety-three feet. A second floor, in addition to boasting "a splendid parlor," contained fifteen "finely furnished rooms."[214] Its façade was of "gray mastic, penciled in imitation of marble blocks and surmounted by heavy cornices with a square finish." The saloon also contained billiard tables crafted in New York, sleeping accommodations and an "architectural elegance, style, character and comfort…not excelled by any similar establishment in California," claimed an advertisement in the 1853–54 *City Directory*. The Magnolia opened on the evening of September 20, 1853, to considerable fanfare, during which "the popping of champagne corks was heard like the regular discharge of musketry from miniature guns."[215] It was the *Democratic Journal*'s contention that the Magnolia, at least at this point in time, was the "oldest one of its kind in this city."[216]

Also part of the post-fire generation of saloons was the Indian Queen. Made of brick and located at 88 J Street between Third and Fourth Streets, it was built at the modest price of $6,000, was two stories high and occupied an area twenty-six feet wide and fifty feet in depth. One particularly colorful passage out of the *Democratic Journal* describes the saloon's reopening after a spring renovation:

A crowd of friends availed themselves yesterday of Professor Daly's invitation to partake of a sumptuous lunch and drinks in honor of the "Indian Queen's" donning her summer dress. A chaste and beauty-dress [sic] it is and reflects great credit on the designer. We called on the proprietor for a mint julep and as we slowly imbibed the delicious compound…it was luscious; the taste remains with us still. If those who partook of mine host's hospitality yesterday continue to call for "daily" drinks at the "Indian Queen," we shall consider it nothing more than he deserves.[217]

The Indian Queen's summertime resurrection also coincided with Daly making permanent his relationship with Miss Mary Davies by marrying her at the city's sole Catholic church, Saint Rose of Lima, in April 1854.

The person of Daly warrants recognition. He was, in a word, dynamic, for while running his Indian Queen, Daly was one of the city's only saloon-owning firemen, served as an alderman for the city's Second Ward in 1854 and was also the first of Sacramento's saloon proprietors to launch branch locations. In addition to the Indian Queen's first annex at Seventh and I Streets (opening in March 1854) and where one could be sure to find "*daily* manipulations of a spirited character," Daly had, concurrently to the branch's debut, opened the Merchant's Exchange Saloon, located in the "What Cheer" building on Front Street, between J and K. He claims to have done so in the *Democratic Journal* "in response to a general demand…for the accommodation of the businessmen on Front Street."[248]

While it was Daly's desire to draw mostly business-class interest, the Exchange and its embarcadero location attracted all types. As the weather improved in late spring 1854, young men, out of work or simply not interested in labor, would race one another on Front Street between K and L for a liquor prize. One particular race, referred to as a "scrub," pitted ten or so men against one another, devil take the hindmost.[249] The sole loser had to pay for the "winners'" drinks, with winnings dispensed at Daly's Merchant's Exchange.

Not letting a good thing languish, Daly rehabilitated the "main branch" of the Indian Queen in September 1854. Descriptions of the opening are quite detailed, including the following from the *Democratic Journal*:

It is most beautifully furnished, being decorated with some sixteen oil paintings. [Daly] has not spared money or time in furnishing his saloon, one single article having cost the round sum of $974. We refer to the magnificent gilt framed mirror. We believe that this is the finest mirror in California.

He regaled his friends on that evening with everything in the way of beverages…in addition to which there was spread a large table…Jim Daly is a most capital fellow; popular and gentlemanly and his friends are "multitude." Success to the new "Indian Queen."[250]

The Indian Queen's facelift came at a time when Daly's political sentiments were drifting from Democrat to Know-Nothing. The Know-Nothings, also referred to as the American Party, were a short-lived, nativist-style movement (1854–56) that, in response to a perceived growth of corruption in urban government, tried to blunt the political influence of Irish Catholic immigrants in major cities. The Know-Nothings, largely composed of middle-class Protestants, were also suspicious of the Vatican, feeling that it was the pope's desire to establish a political network of loyal Catholics throughout the United States and thereby influence public policy. Daly's declaration for the Know-Nothings, as well as his desire to see like-minded politicos at the Indian Queen, was made in few uncertain terms in November 1854: "KNOW NOTHINGS AND FREEDOM'S PHALANX ATTEND!"[251]

One of the most influential post-fire upstarts was the Fashion, a place whose prospects matched the panache of its name. Established sometime in November 1852, the Fashion sat at 39 J Street. Its Irish-born owner, John C. Keenan, was described by the *Union* as that "incomparable leader of the mode…[Keenan]…whose taste for the outer and inner adornment of man is acknowledged to be the sine qua non of excellence."[252] One intriguing aspect of Keenan's pre-Sacramento life involved his role with the fabled Texas Rangers, a fighting force born out of early efforts to protect Texans from Indian attacks and incursions by Mexico.[253] The bulk of the Rangers' reputation, however, was earned with their performance in the Mexican War of 1846–48, under the leadership of the legendary Captain John Coffee "Jack" Hays. Ireland may have been Keenan's birthplace, but he appears to have made a home in Texas, where he arrived in the spring of 1849 via Mexico. After doing so, he became a Ranger. Specifics are scant on Keenan's part in the group, but we do know that he served under Hays after the war with Mexico had ended and prior to departing for California.

After the November fire, the energetic Keenan sensed opportunity and raced to the now-extinct city of Vernon, located at the confluence of the Sacramento and Feather Rivers. Once there, he purchased a prefabricated wooden structure and floated it to Sacramento.[254] The new saloon then bowed out of the city's cultural scene for a six-month period,

Shown here along J Street circa 1960, the Fashion was started by ex–Texas Ranger John C. Keenan. *Library of Congress.*

returning in April after a "complete rejuvenation…fully emerged from its chrysalis state."[255]

Keenan possessed more on his daily docket than just the Fashion. While a member of the Sutter Rifles and treasurer of Engine Company No.5, his primary diversion came as manager of the Sutter Race Grounds, located east of the city "between the old Stockton and Jackson Roads, near Harrigan's Two Friends House."[256] At the time of the Gold Rush, horse racing's

American pedigree was already quite rich. Brought over to the eastern United States from England and France, the sport seamlessly meshed with the country's agrarian roots, and as the population shifted westward, so too did racing. The first few regional tracks to open, San Francisco's Pioneer Course and Sacramento's own Brighton Jockey Club, did so in 1851. Races at the Sutter Race Grounds debuted in the spring of 1854 and included two horses owned by none other than John Frederick Morse, they being Lilly and Trifle.

A direct competitor to the Sutter was the Louisiana Race Track, located at what is now Twelfth Avenue and Franklin Boulevard, an area also known as Whiskey Hill because of the presence of two saloons. The Louisiana, managed by C.S. Ellis, opened for business in early 1855 as a trotting and racing course. For one dollar, spectators, many of whom came from as far as San Francisco, were granted access to all parts of the course. Ellis's management style, however, came under criticism as he was accused of running a slipshod operation fraught with "a series of starts, balks, humbugs and tomfooleries that would disgust anyone who ever saw or had any idea of how such things should be properly conducted."[257] The *Democratic Journal*'s criticism was not without solution as it suggested that the Louisiana management visit Keenan's Sutter Course to view "horse racing done up as it should be."[258]

The Sutter and Louisiana tracks were direct descendants of the colorfully named Brighton Jockey Club. The BJC's arrival was big news to many of

The Louisiana Racetrack had its own saloon and eventually became home to the California State Fair. *Center for Sacramento History.*

the newly transplanted race enthusiasts from the east. Its grounds were massive, covering no less than 130 acres. The Brighton's stewards, most notably John Sutter Sr., celebrated the track's opening with an inaugural ball at the Orleans House in May 1851. When up and running, the track offered races in increments of one, two or three miles for four-leggers like Wake-Up-Jake, Wisconsin Chief, Lem Gustin, Black Swan, Cock Robin and Whalebone, to name a few. The BJC enjoyed a favorable run and was known to draw up to 2,500 spectators for a single event. However, in February 1852, it was plowed into a barley field, "leaving no traces of the track over which the fleet coursers so lately sped."[259] The earliest harvest from the newly planted grain was claimed by the *Union* to "have surpassed any we have seen the present season," growing some six feet, eight inches in length.[260]

The Alhambra Saloon opened its doors in late December 1852 at 67 J Street, near Third Street, "phenix [*sic*] like, arisen from the ashes and still afloat."[261] L.N. Gibson of Pennsylvania was its proprietor, but his wife, Josephine, seemed to be the one who truly made the saloon go. Like Radford's, the Alhambra was keen on serving up oysters "in every style."[262] It was also one of many saloons that offered ice cream, especially during the summer months. Upon receiving a gift of the sweet confection from Josephine, the *Democratic Journal* claimed that "the thermometer" fell "twenty degrees in the office upon its arrival."[263] The Alhambra started strong—strong enough to open a branch in the temporary village of Hoboken. However, by the spring of 1853, the Alhambra's tenor changed. In July, the saloon was up for sale, the owner "desirous of leaving California."[264]

In a notable twist, Mr. Gibson was not speaking for Mrs. Gibson. Josephine, also referred to as "Old Joe," chose to stay in Sacramento, opening her own saloon on February 22, 1854, on Second Street across from the Wells Fargo and Company Express Office. The Capital Saloon, not to be confused with a business of the same name on J Street between Sixth and Seventh Streets, was a significant newcomer for one particular reason: it was owned by a woman, making it one of the first female-owned saloons in the city's history.

In addition to a full bar, the Capital ensured "oyster stews, fried oysters, shelled oysters and clams, ham and eggs, tea and coffee and ice creams in season."[265] Josephine's strengths were not simply culinary; she could also draft a catchy poem, as evidenced in one of the more amusing advertisements for Sacramento victuals out of the November 21, 1854 *California Statesman*:

LEVI HERMANCE,

Attorney and Counselor-at-Law,

Office, K Street, between 6th and 7th, Sacramento.

ATLANTIC CABLE SALOON

J Street, between Eleventh and Twelfth,

SACRAMENTO.

Choice LIQUORS and CIGARS always on hand. Also, comfortable LODGING ROOMS.   L. PRESTON, Proprietor.

ORIENTAL SALOON,

CORNER OF I AND SEVENTH STS.,

SACRAMENTO.

☞ The above Saloon is furnished with the choicest LIQUORS and CIGARS.   McKEON, Proprietor.

ILLINOIS HOTEL,

J Street, between Tenth and Eleventh,

SACRAMENTO.

In connection with this Hotel there is a BAR and large BILLIARD SALOON.   JOHN MERKER, Proprietor.

Overland-Mail Saloon,

J Street, between Twelfth and Thirteenth,

SACRAMENTO.

CHOICE LIQUORS AND SEGARS always on hand.

SAMUEL F. ROBINETT, Proprietor.

Whether in homage to mail delivery or international communication, it was common for saloons to take on the names of trending events. *Sacramento Public Library.*

OYSTERS! OYSTERS!
FRESH OYSTERS, ALL PRIME,
To be served in quick time,
Either roasted or fried,
Stewed, pickled or pied,
As gentlemen wish
Who call for a dish;
Whigs, Democrats, Know-Nothings and all,
Please give us a call.[266]

By December 1855, Josephine had moved her saloon into a larger building formerly occupied by the Arcade Saloon, on 40 and 42 J Street, naming it, most fittingly, Josey's Saloon.

Gibson wasn't Sacramento's sole female saloon owner. In fact, throughout the 1850s and early 1860s, we know that area saloons came under the ownership of at least nine other women.[267] Jeanette Frank, Elizabeth Cooper, Betsey Bennet, Anne Marie Walteamath, Elizabeth Chappell, Bridget Hunt, Catherine Little and Sarah Oakley all held sole trader status as operators, meaning they formed the single, independent, decision-making entity for their businesses. The Eagle Saloon, located on Second Street near K, was under the sole operation of Mrs. T.C. Trotter. In addition to its full complement of liquors, the Eagle claimed to serve "viands…in such a manner as 'to please the taste of the most fastidious.'"[268] The English-born Trotter was a youngish twentysomething at the time of the saloon's opening in 1853.

Despite the presence of these accomplished female saloon operators, the overall presence of women in city saloons, although not uncommon, had to have been outside the norm (proprietors or prostitutes notwithstanding). In 1850, women accounted for one out of every twelve California immigrants. In 1860, the number of female immigrants increased, although still amounting to only one out of three new Californians.[269]

Though almost exclusively incubators of manhood, saloons were not without female accommodation. Some spots, like the Orleans, provided the "ladies' ordinary," referred to in another source as "the wineroom in the back."[270] It was also said to be the first of its kind in the Sacramento area.[271] The ordinary sought to sequester women from the standard bar area while providing so much of what was being enjoyed in the saloon proper. Moreover, because the thought of ladies pushing their way through the sacred "batwings" was not quite yet a palatable one to a large slice of the male population, more than one establishment created alternate or private entrances. Once in the saloon's ordinary, women could eat, drink and leisurely chat away the hours.

In the less posh saloons of the city, women appear to have been treated as viable front door–entering customers. What is more, gender had no mitigating effect on a woman's ability—like her male counterpart—to get drunk and disorderly. Charlotte King's late summer 1861 drinking binge resulted in the discharge "of a pistol at a gambler, named Brooks, but without striking the object aimed at."[272] After she was dragged, kicking and screaming, from the saloon at Sixth and K, it was King's contention that Brooks had cheated her out of ten dollars in a game of rondo. When Brooks attempted to remove King, she pulled the weapon from her "bosom" and fired wide of the lucky gambler.

We should also mention that women moved about Alta California with a certain measure of comfort. As historian John Boessenecker states, "Because they were so scarce, most Forty-Niners treated women not just with respect but with reverence, for they represented the mothers, sisters, daughters, wives, and sweethearts left at home."[273] Corroborating as much, between 1850 and 1861, nearly fifty-one men—statewide—were convicted and sent to San Quentin on charges of rape or attempted rape. Placed in a modern context, raw statistics would tell us that women are five times more likely to have violence perpetrated against them in the twenty-first century than during the Gold Rush era. It is perhaps the case that the same level of safety followed the female form into many of Sacramento's Gold Rush saloons.

The Blue Wing also burst onto the saloon scene as a strong purveyor of the mixed drink or the cocktail, a uniquely American invention of the nineteenth century whose etymological origins go back to roughly 1803. Owned by Louisiana transplant E.L. Smith, the Wing, in the old confines of the Gem, stood at the corner of J and Second Streets at 29 J Street. Its name came from a distinctive characteristic of the golden eagle surmounting the entrance of the saloon: it possessed one blue wing. Smith's menu of cocktails was diverse: Roman punch, lemon punch, mountaineers, strawberry juleps, pineapple punch, hock and sherry cobblers were just a few of them.

Turnbull's, owned by Robert Turnbull, was located on Second Street. It was the first of Sacramento's saloons to offer a drink known as the "Mountaineer." The drink's inventor—or so he claimed—was J.B. Brouilette from Louisiana. It is unclear what ingredients made up a Mountaineer, but a more modern version is composed of one ounce of orange juice, a quarter ounce of lemon juice, a half ounce of ginger ale, one and a half ounces rum, a quarter ounce of milk and one teaspoon of pepper. It appears that the drink was so popular that a Sacramento saloon located on K between Third and Fourth chose to name itself accordingly. In addition to spirits, Turnbull's retained the services of a "superior French cook" who went far in ensuring a lunch table "supplied with the choicest Viands in the market."[274]

The Marion House opened its doors in early December 1852 under the guidance of J.W. Stillman. Located at 43 J Street between Second and Third Streets, the Marion boasted full bar fixtures, fifteen rooms for lodging and six billiard tables with "balls and cues, always in good order."[275] The Marion seemed to possess an edge, one harkening back to the grittier days of the Mansion House. Such was the case on the evening of April 3, 1854. A number of men were sitting in the saloon, discussing a row that had taken place earlier in the day at Second and K's Verandah. Things heated up when George McDonald, a baker from England, and James Turner exchanged "high words."[276] Near tragedy took place when McDonald took his pistol and fired a bullet into the back of Turner, entering "at the point of the left shoulder blade and ranging across the back, lodg[ing] inside the skin of the neck above the right shoulder." After falling, Turner was carried to the drugstore of a Mr. Simmons at 48½ J Street. The *Union* reported the bullet to have been extracted not fifteen minutes after entering Turner's body, allowing him to experience a smooth recovery. Two years earlier, in August 1852, the incorrigible Turner had been involved in a shooting at the Diana. When refusing to pay for his liquor, the saloon's bartender "went to the end of the counter, got a revolver and discharged three or four shots at Turner," one of which lodged in his neck. After being taken to San Francisco for the cooler weather, Turner went on to recover.[277]

A markedly more passive event at the Marion House, a qualified hook, took place in the spring of 1855 when Eclipse the "mammoth ox" was showcased to Sacramento's most curious. According to advertisements, the six-year-old Eclipse weighed two tons and was purported to be the "largest animal in the United States." It cost fifty cents for one's bovine curiosity to be satisfied.[278]

The Marion's clear trump in violence was the Arcade, located on J Street. The saloon debuted in January 1855 and did so looking for a fight.[279] The first row occurred on January 13 between Charles Brockaway and D.C. Henderson. The latter was quietly playing cards when Brockaway jumped in and seized hold of Henderson's money. As Henderson spewed "vile epithets," Brockaway grabbed a stool "and so on." Eventually, a police officer stepped in, separating the two. For their trouble, both men were fined twenty dollars each. Just days later, H. Whitcomb was enjoying his dinner in the Arcade when Owen McKim strolled into the saloon and "applied a most disgusting epithet to him."[280] With ire raised, Whitcomb retaliated with a "'sog dologer' in the frontpiece of Owen, which completely floored him." Just as Whitcomb was about to take a stool to McKim, the police entered the saloon, arresting both men and fining them each twenty dollars. While Whitcomb was able to pay, it was reported that "McKim will probably have to work his passage." A week later at the Arcade, William Barnes and J.P. Dillon "got up an exhibition of pugilistic powers" resulting in the arrest of both, but a stiffer penalty of twenty-five dollars was assessed to each.[281] By mid-February, the *Democratic Journal* had had enough, claiming, "If rowdyism continues to increase in this saloon in the same ratio of the week past, public interest will require it be indicted as a nuisance."[282]

The Arcade, however, lived because of its insatiability to a bevy of curious customers. The public could not deny its gambling allure, and the case of a very common figure in James Gudgeon illustrates as much.[283] Gudgeon, a carpenter by trade and far from being a professional gambler, was reported by the *California Statesman* to have, on one Friday night, "bucked a little at faro." After quickly losing $250, he turned to the dealer, a man named Barr, calling him a "thief." Barr then "bunged his eye with a blow of his fist." When the dust cleared, Gudgeon "came out decidedly second best, having a black eye, a broken finger and other minor injuries." In front of the county recorder the following day, Gudgeon was fined $30 and Barr $40 "and trimmings for their pugnacity."

Moving from brawling to brewing, an often-heard term during this time in Sacramento, especially when the weather warmed, was "lager beer." The term applied to a style of beer and the name of more than one drinking establishment in the city. The lager-style drink originated in the Bavarian region of southeastern Germany and made its way to the United States in 1842. By the time of the Gold Rush, the lager—both within California and out—had become a popular alternative to the more traditional ale, so much so that in the fall of 1854, when the community of St. Louis ran out of lager beer, the headline of the *Democratic Journal's* story on the crisis read "Horrible."[284] According to the same article, in the six months previous, St. Louis consumed an estimated eighteen million glasses of lager.

The term lager comes from the German verb *lagern*, meaning "to store." After fermentation, lagers are typically aged for several weeks, even months, at a temperature of nearly fifty degrees Fahrenheit, sometimes cooler. The process helps leach yeasts and proteins, both of which effectively mellow the beer's taste. As we remember, ales, the standard beer up to the advent of the lager, are brewed both more quickly and at a higher temperature. One true lover of the lager-style beer was California's third governor, John Bigler, who was known to carry powdered soda and magnesia in his chest pocket to keep his stomach settled as he imbibed his brew.

Sacramento's introduction to regionally brewed, lager-style beer came in the spring of 1853. The product was shipped from San Francisco and sold from a saloon located within Heywood's Building on the corner of J and Second Streets. The San Francisco Saloon, originally known as the Beer and Billiards Saloon, of Germans Edward Kleibitz and Robert Green, on Fourth Street between J and K, also acquired brew from San Francisco's Jacob Gundlach and his Bavaria Brewery in San Francisco. The debut of locally produced lager came in 1854 when Louis Keseberg opened the Phoenix Brewery at the southeast corner of Twenty-eighth and M Streets. Originally nothing more than a barroom, the refit Phoenix made an immediate impact on Sacramento. Not only did it establish a tasting room at 324 J Street, between Tenth and Eleventh Streets, but as described by the *Democratic Journal* in May, the Phoenix took alcohol marketing to a whole new level: "A new beer wagon, intended for the Brewery at the Fort, was paraded through the principal streets about ten o'clock last night, drawn by about fifty men and followed by a thirsty crowd. A pole was upreared [*sic*] from the center, bearing an American ensign, stiffened in the breeze and a band of music

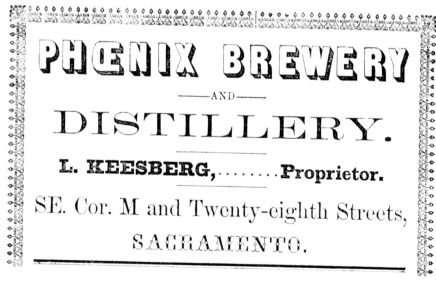

Louis Keseberg went from starvation with the Donner Party to opening up his own brewery, the Phoenix, in 1854. *Sacramento Public Library.*

occupied the broad surface of the truck. There was probably a noisy time at the irrigation which was contemplated."[285]

As sales increased and the brewery expanded, prices dropped from seventy-five cents to a tasty sixty-five cents per gallon. In July, the *Journal* extolled the Phoenix's "most excellent drink…supplying daily, hundreds of our citizens—they make nothing but the pure article."[286]

In August 1856, Keseberg was arrested for assaulting an individual who entered the brewery. The intruder was reported to have threatened a Phoenix employee, but after Keseberg ordered him to leave the premises, a row ensued. Days later, the owner was forced to answer before the county recorder. The brewer's "unbridled temper," not to mention his questionable past, both stand worthy of discussion.[287] Described by Heinrich Lienhard as "a tall, intelligent man of military bearing," Keseberg was born in Prussia and came to the United States in 1844 with his wife, Phillipine. His decision to head to California forever connected him to one of the more infamous migratory disasters in American history, the Donner Party.[288] Reports paint a character in Keseberg as anything but stable, adding that he possessed a "rapid, loud and 'somewhat excited' manner of speech." The brewer was also accused by several emigrants of beating his wife.[289] What's more, near the beginning of the party's journey, Keseberg was suspected of killing a fellow emigrant, a man named Wolfinger, for his money in the fall of 1846.[290]

Topping off the brewer's sinister aura was the claim—by many—that he was the first person in the Donner Party to resort to cannibalism. In any case, after evading justice and then embarking on assorted ventures, including one as a riverboat captain, Keseberg settled in Sacramento and opened the Phoenix. In spite of his cannibalistic past, lager lovers didn't give

Prussian-born Louis Keseberg was known to have a bit of an anger problem. *Sacramento Public Library.*

things a second thought—the Phoenix brew sold well. By late summer 1858, the brewery was turning out nearly 1,500 gallons of lager a week.[291]

With the Phoenix well aloft, several businesses were eager to retail the brewery's lager. J.H.C. Waltemath's Lager Beer Saloon opened in May 1854 on the south side of J Street near Eighth Street, and Joseph Brown's Lager Beer and Chop Saloon opened at 38 J Street in November, offering the "Best LAGER BEER in Sacramento."[292] In July, Henry Eisenmenger and H. Ehman opened the Sacramento Beer Cellar in the basement of a brick building on J between Sixth and Seventh Streets. It is described as "well-furnished and bountifully supplied with that excellent article, Lager Beer, with which the friends of the proprietors were regaled...with as much as they could drink." The Cellar also served lunch and provided music through the company of a "fine brass band."[293] Appearing, by all accounts, above ground was the Lager Bier and Coffee Saloon on Second Street, between J and K. M. Elias, originally of New York, was the proprietor. In addition to "steaks, chops, etc, etc," Elias offered a "Sacred Concert every Sunday evening."[294]

Sacramento's appreciation of the lager beer was a profoundly transnational one, as relayed by the *Democratic Journal*:

> *Germans and their direct descendants seemed, a short time ago, the only persons who appreciated its particular flavor, but now it is the drink of all sorts of conditions of men, from those who claim it as their national liquid down to the elliptical-eyed Celestials and dingy-hued Californians. Lager beer saloons are numerous on "J" Street; there is one at nearly every corner...The professional man, the merchant, the mechanic, the clerk; all are contracting a passion for the Lager Beer saloon and its concomitants.*[295]

Lager's cool, refreshing taste gave it an advantage over the heavier ale, more commonly consumed at room temperature. The location of lager-serving saloons in cooled cellars, especially during Sacramento's summer months, proves far from surprising. With cooling technology still in its infancy, cellars were a cost-effective way to keep one's product fresh and drinkable. It was not until 1859 that we have any indicator of an individual saloon utilizing an "ice closet" to store its lager beer. Klay's Saloon, located on Fourth, between J and K, drew from its closet lager of the "best quality...as though it were ice itself."[296]

Still, if one chose to stay at ground level, there were refrigeration options. The Sitka Ice House, located on Front and I Streets, was built at an estimated cost of $11,000 and featured double-thick, charcoal-lined

CALIFORNIA ICE COMPANY.

Office, THIRD STREET, between I and J,

(HILLER & ANDREWS' BLOCK,)

SACRAMENTO CITY.

☞ The undersigned beg to inform the citizens of Sacramento and vicinity, that having preserved a sufficient quantity of

Ice of California Product,

With Depots at PILOT CREEK, GEORGETOWN, COLOMA, AUBURN, PLACERVILLE, JACKSON, GRANITE CITY and SACRAMENTO, they are prepared to guarantee supplies throughout the Season, at the universal price of **Seven cts. per pound.**

TALLMAN & REED,

PROPRIETORS.

An enjoyable lager beer needed to be cold, and if Sacramento was not pulling its ice out of the Sierra Nevadas, it was buying it from companies that imported chunks from Alaska. The California Ice Company was one such company. *Sacramento Public Library.*

walls.[297] It was intended to hold up to one thousand tons of ice. When opening in the spring of 1854, each one-pound increment of ice was sold for ten cents. The Sitka's presence was a revelation for saloons that, if not opting to cellar their goods, were required to venture into the Sierra Nevada for ice. The product, obtained from what was then the Russian territory of Alaska, was considered by the 1856 *City Directory* to be of "excellent quality and can be obtained at all seasons of the years."[298] An ice provider to follow the Sitka was the California Ice Company on Third Street, between I and J Streets.

The Columbus Brewery, located on the corner of K and Sixteenth Streets, started lager production in 1853 under the guidance of brothers Elias and Christian Grühler, both hailing from the Baden-Wurttemberg region of

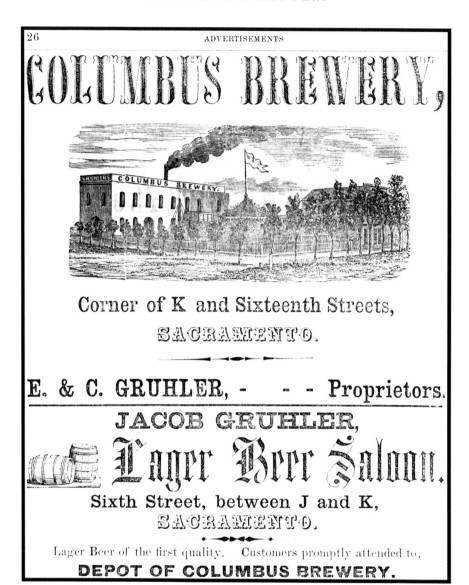

COLUMBUS BREWERY,

Corner of K and Sixteenth Streets, SACRAMENTO.

E. & C. GRUHLER, - - - Proprietors.

JACOB GRUHLER,

Lager Beer Saloon.

Sixth Street, between J and K, SACRAMENTO.

Lager Beer of the first quality.   Customers promptly attended to.

DEPOT OF COLUMBUS BREWERY.

An advertisement for the Columbus Brewery and its primary retailer, the Lager Beer Saloon, from the 1857 *City Directory*. *Courtesy of the Sacramento Room Archives.*

Germany. By 1858, they were making 1,200 gallons of beer per week.[299] At full production, the Grühlers employed two to three men to operate the tubs, as well as a cooper to construct barrels. Their primary distribution point was the Grühler Saloon, located on Sixth Street, between J and K.

As the summer of 1853 descended upon Sacramento, the city found itself hosting a solid crop of 139 bars or drinking saloons, a far cry from the 208 recorded in 1851, but still a robust number considering the presence of fire not ten months earlier.[300] Moreover, the city's liquor wholesaling community had found some traction. By December, William A. McWilliams and Company, by all indications the city's largest seller of alcohol, had reopened for business at 22 K Street between Second and Front. Its list of offerings, almost all imported, is impressive: Martel, London Dock and Otard brandies; claret; hock; sherry; champagne; Irish malt, Scotch and Monongahela whiskeys; Holland Gin; Jamaican rum; English ale; and porter. Even Guinness's Dublin Porter could be found there.[301] Other local sellers of alcohol included William Walker and Company at 115 J Street, between Fourth and Fifth; Despecher and Field at 57 J Street; and J.D. Mairs and Company on 97 K Street near the corner of Fourth Street.

As can be seen, the saloon community's post-fire renaissance was a heady one. However, not all Sacramentans were pleased. The Whiggish *Union* exhibited its consternation by writing: "These places of resort will spring up, though never a church or dwelling house were built in the city. To see the number of decanters of bad liquor arrayed on dirty boards, with scarcely a shelter to cover them, would lead a citizen of Maine [referring to Maine's prohibition legislation] to suppose that guzzling was the great object and aim of life in Sacramento. A little reform in this respect would be quite a credit to the city."[302]

Based on the impact of the 1852 fire, as well as a crescendo of events on the national scene, it was easy to see why prohibitionists had hope. In 1851, the state of Maine became the first member of the Union to outlaw the manufacture and sale of intoxicating liquors within its borders. By 1855, thirteen of thirty-one states committed themselves to similar legislation. The news proved momentous for Sacramento teetotalers, prompting the city's local chapter of the Sons of Temperance to both publish Maine's liquor law and furnish California's governor and each of the state's assembly and senate members with a copy.

The Maine legislation inspired a series of lectures, meetings, demonstrations and several "dry" meetings. The most extensive display of good, clean temperance fun took place in late December 1853 under the guidance of the city's Sons and Daughters of Temperance. The *Union* reported the party to possess "no lack of hilarity, vivacity, or of a free and full flow of life and spirit from the absence of wines, etc.," and included that "the demonstration should satisfy us that intoxicating beverages are not absolutely essential to cheer the festive board."[303]

In addition to the Sons and Daughters of Temperance, Sacramento became home to the youth-centered Cadets of Temperance in January 1852 and then in May 1853. Though separate in name, all groups met in the confines of the same place: Temperance Hall, located at 52 K Street. It was here that those intent on guiding public policy discussed the prospect of entering local and state politics. The first such effort was powered by a caucus held in March 1854. By April, Sacramento teetotalers had chosen Ben Essely for mayor. Josephine Gibson, proprietor of the Capital Saloon, was perhaps even feeling some impact of the prohibitionist traction, declaring that "the triumph of temperance has not caused [her] to 'fizzle out,' but [she] is 'still at home,' 'alive and kicking' and with the largest supply of the purest and oldest liquors in the vicinity of the Capital."[304]

After the state legislature passed an act in May 1855 entitled "To Take the Sense of the People of This State…on the Passage of Prohibitory Liquor Law," the temperance community was afforded a chance to see the effect of its lobbying efforts. In mid-September, the county voted on a liquor law that would "prohibit the manufacture and sale of all spirituous and intoxicating liquors, except for mechanical, chemical, medicinal and Sacramental purposes."[305] The results—2,195–1,493 against prohibition—were revealing. Sacramento was, at its heart, a truly "wet" city.[306] The *Democratic Journal* referred to Sacramento as being decidedly in favor of the "ardent," a reference to the oft-used term "ardent spirits." It also was reported in the *Union* that, since the passage of the Maine Liquor Law, Rhode Island's demand for "ardent spirits" had increased by 20 percent.[307] Sacramento's Sons of Temperance lamented the loss in the form of a torchlight procession in October 1855. Heading the group of 120 was a brass band that, starting at the corner of J and Tenth Streets, finished at the Reverend Benton's church (Pioneer Congregational Church).[308]

In the decade's latter years, efforts to restrain the sale and consumption of alcohol were recurring but generally ineffectual. Perhaps the most extensive and meaningful piece of temperance legislation was enacted in 1858, capping the amount of money to be paid for "the purchase of, or the sale and delivery of any spirituous or malt liquors, wine or cider, by retail or by drink" at five dollars.[309] It sought to curb binging, as well as the proliferation of debt, vis-à-vis saloon accounts. The *Union* approved of the act, calling it a way to "keep the picks in the hands of miners and laborers and a good deal of poison in the bottles of shopkeepers."[310]

Gaming's time of reckoning had also come. Senator William C. Hoff, a Democrat from San Francisco, introduced a bill that sought the suppression and license of public gaming in general. In March 1851, anti-gambling proponents could finally experience some success on a statewide level when "An Act to License Gaming" passed both houses, making it high season for "mining the gamblers." The law's primary impact rested in the jurisdiction that it gave counties, requiring gaming houses to apply for—and purchase—licensing from county treasurers.

Licenses weren't cheap by any stretch. For every three months, the licensee was required to pay $1,500 for three or more tables and $1,000 for fewer than three. The assessment applied only to San Francisco, Sacramento and Marysville, with other jurisdictions paying a markedly more reasonable $35 per month per table. Three-quarters of licensing revenue went into the state budget and one-fourth into county coffers. The act also allowed municipalities to perform further licensing and assessment as they saw fit. Also affecting the gaming landscape was the criminalization of French monte, thimblerig and lotteries, three J Street standards. The penalty for hosting the illicit games included three to six months in jail and a fine of between $500 and $2,000. Provisions of the act did not extend to billiards or bowling.[311]

In August 1852, one campaign sought the prohibition of public gambling on Sundays. "When will the citizens of Sacramento see the day when public gaming on the Lord's Day will be suppressed?" asked the *Union*'s editorial voice, "Moralicus."[312] Though San Francisco, Marysville and Stockton all would enact laws to protect the Sabbath during this time, Sacramento would not follow suit until a few years later. Flaccid efforts like the proposed Sabbath ban proved the norm until the overall fortunes of gaming opponents seemed to look up in April 1855, when Governor Bigler signed into law a bill banning most banking games. In essence, anyone brave enough to open or cause "any gaming bank or game of chance…may be prosecuted by indictment by the Grand Jury of the county in which the offense shall have been committed."[313] In a turnabout from the 1851 law, billiards and bowling also fell under the bill's purview.

Next, "upon evidence of one or more credible witnesses," penalties assessed to persons "who shall deal" would not exceed $500, nor would they be less than $100 for the first offense. The same penalty applied to the owner of the gaming establishment unless it could be proven that he or she had no knowledge of the illicit act. Fine disbursement ensured that one-fourth of the revenue went to the district attorney of the county in which the offense was committed, one-fourth to the county's treasury and the remaining sum being "equally divided among the various Orphan Asylums in counties where such Asylums exist and where there are no such Asylums, shall go into the 'General School Fund' of the county." The act then ensured that "all notes, bills, bonds, mortgages or other securities or conveyances whatever" involved in wagering "shall be void and of no effect."[314] With the new legislation also repealing both the March 1851 "Act to License Gaming" and its April 1851 amendment, a huge dimension of public gaming in California was dead, with the personality of Sacramento and the general state's saloon culture slowly reflecting as much.

As we've learned, the Arcade represented the very den that vice legislation meant to control or kill. The demise of John Reed, most of his fall having occurred in the infamous Arcade during the lead-up to prohibition, seems to have been a lightning rod for public anger and a clear illustration of gambling's insidious effects. Reed, a twenty-two-year-old native of Steubenville, Ohio, was an employee of the *State Journal* and was well loved by colleagues, "esteemed for the generosity and affability of his disposition." His darker tendencies led him toward "the hell on 'J' Street known as the Arcade," where repeated losses and consequential liabilities left Reed penniless. The gravity of his indiscretions proved so unbearable that he opted to commit suicide through the ingestion of strychnine. The most chilling vestige of Reed's fall came in the form of his farewell letter: "I HAVE RUINED MYSELF FOREVER BY GAMBLING AND THE APPETITE I HAVE FORMED FOR THE PERNICIOUS HABIT IS SO STRONG THAT I FIND IT IMPOSSIBLE TO QUIT."[315]

Shaped by stories like that of Reed's, the role of public sentiment in the suppression of gaming cannot be overstated. Sacramento and the state as a whole were growing to be more demographically and economically heterogeneous; the days of service outlets accommodating solely the reckless whims of miners, young and old, were supplanted by an era in which merchants, laborers and even families were demanding to be heard. The state's demographic footprint in 1854–55 was clearly different from what it was just a few years earlier. As of late August 1850, it was reported that nearly 43,000 immigrants came through Fort Laramie; 92 percent of them were male, while the remaining 8 percent were women and children.[316] The state's population for that year was 92,597.[317] Two years later, the state's population crested at 255,122.[318] Of this number, most residents were between the ages of twenty and forty, and over 90 percent were male.[319] Before the end of 1853, however, 70 percent of those who arrived by sea between 1849 and 1853 (roughly 175,000 people) had left the same way.[320] This dramatic shift—the departure of so many young men and, with it, the demand for drink and game—had a remarkable effect on the state's saloon culture. In short, with the ebb of the Gold Rush, California was finally settling, as were its demands for vice. As stated by historian John M. Findlay, "Californians gradually redefined gaming as beyond the borders of respectability as they set about taming their society."[321]

It is also true that the anti-gaming community sought to eliminate the longstanding fraternity of professional gamblers. Figures like Charles Cora symbolized a perceived scourge. Moralists, hoping to infuse puritanical East Coast ideas of right and wrong into California society, saw professional gamers as not simply outside the "borders of respectability" but as a clear threat to who and what guided the ethical and political compass of a community. In a situation similar to what followed the demise of Frederick Roe, a San Francisco Vigilance Committee sprang forth in November 1855 after Cora shot U.S. Marshal William H. Richard, supposedly in an effort to bolster Democrat James Y. McDuffie's chances to be appointed to the then-open marshal's position. The tacit voice of the committee was newspaper editor James King of William. Because of Cora's association with McDuffie (both had gambled professionally in Marysville), it was King's contention that gamers were colluding with Democrats to take control of the state. Although McDuffie freely acknowledged a brief career as a gambler during a time when it was a licensed and somewhat acceptable endeavor, he denied any connection to Cora. For taking a stand, King was himself assassinated in May 1856 by rival editor James P. Casey. King was quickly martyred to the anti-gambling cause, giving his committee sufficient moral leverage to hang Casey and Cora, both of whom were executed on May 22, 1856. In effect, Cora's death proved to be a metaphor for change, for soon, instead of being looked upon as temples of glamour and escape, as they had been in 1850, gaming halls and their masters were viewed as roadblocks to social development.[322]

In Sacramento, public sentiment regarding King's demise was profound. When the editor finally succumbed, church and fire engine bells rang throughout the river city, businessmen closed their stores for portions of the day and flags were hung at half-mast. Even the opposition, *Democratic State Journal*, conceded that King "was a vigorous writer and…correct in all his social relations. He is dead and malice is disarmed." The paper did, however, question the unlawful executions of Cora and Casey: "We must have law; we must have courts of justice to settle the thousand disagreements which daily arise in society."[323] Not surprisingly, the *Union* (and again, reminiscent of the Roe debacle) sided with the committee, feeling that "law is defined to be a rule of action presented by the supreme power. The people are the

James Casey takes aim at rival newspaper editor James King of William. The latter's death proved a watershed event for California gambling. *Sacramento Public Library.*

supreme power, with us and when they calmly determine that their agents are unworthy of their confidence, that self preservation requires it, they have the right to re-organize upon the principles of democracy and administer justice and punish crime."[324]

It is notable that while state legislation outlawed the *hosting* of most banking games, it neglected to assign equal penalty for *playing* such games. This element seems to typify the irresolute character of much of California's anti-gaming legislation during the decade, which, according to Findlay, "did not outlaw every kind of game, proved difficult to enforce and provided mainly light penalties. Government found it hard to deter citizens from wagering at their favorite diversion, for gaming was deeply ingrained in the population."[325]

Although not much documentation exists on the Metropolitan Saloon, an amusing anecdote speaks, in part, to Findlay's point that Californians would gamble habitually, regardless of legality or, in this case, common sense. It involved a bet at the Metropolitan between two miners on their adeptness "at throwing a missile at a mark."[326] The bet amounted to $1.50 and would hinge on who "could hit the large mirror behind the bar with a lager beer glass thrown from a distance of 20 feet." Within seconds, "the lager beer glass crashed into the mirror and made it a wreck of broken reflections."[327] The happy thrower claimed his winnings, more than pleased to pay the $170 required to replace the mirror. An equally telling story comes from the November 20, 1860 *Union*, which talks about the gaming activities of pupils at Franklin School who "spend a considerable portion of their time with a dice box in playing poker-dice for marbles. They appear to be lamentably familiar with the rules and slang phrases of the gaming table and may possibly be contracting a stronger taste for dice than for books."[328]

Concurrently, we see a growing number of diversions in Sacramento pulling citizens out of gaming houses. Stockton, for example, in April 1854, rejoiced in the closure of its version of the El Dorado on the corner of Centre and Levee: "Yesterday, carpenters were engaged in dividing its capacious dimensions into stores…Within the past year much has been accomplished toward placing our city in a healthier and higher position than heretofore. The great accession to our female population and children has done so much in influencing these results—school houses and churches have taken the place of gaming saloons."[329]

The same refit of gaming saloons was occurring to the north as well. In late 1854, the El Dorado, once the city's "overwhelming gambling vortex," was put to use "for better purposes" as it became the home to Keyes and Company Clothiers and Collins and Company Hatters, which instead of dealing cards was dealing hats made of "Rocky Mountain Beaver." By this time, Rueben Raynes was fully out of the picture, now placing his efforts into the Fashion. Eli Skaggs, a twentysomething from Missouri, took control of the El Dorado at the price of $30,000.[330]

By virtue of a license it had received from Sacramento County, the Arcade was able to continue its gaming operations through July 1, 1855. Arcadians (a term referring to those operating or frequenting the saloon), perhaps attempting to diversify their offerings and ceremoniously open a new chapter in their history, hosted a "ball" on July 11. It was interrupted by an all too common altercation between two men that resulted in arrests and the shooting of a policeman.[331] When the saloon finally did close, James J. Rawls erected a two-story brick building in its place, its new role being that of a market for the sale of meat and vegetables.

With the swoon of gaming, several more wholesome diversions scurried forth to entertain Sacramento. Theaters were a well-established alternative. By 1855, the Forrest and Sacramento Theaters were showing everything from *Macbeth* to *Brutus*, starring the earlier-mentioned Edwin Booth. By

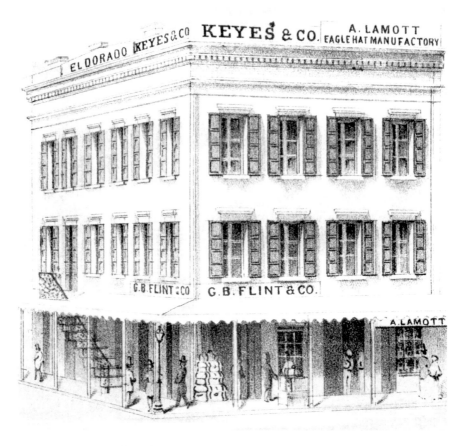

The last incarnation of the El Dorado Building, which went from gambling den to business center. *Center for Sacramento History.*

December 1853, Sacramento had its own debate and lecture club, the Lyceum, which tackled compelling questions of the day like: "Would the donation of public lands by Congress for building the Atlantic and Pacific Railroad be legal and expedient?"[332]; "Would it be expedient and Constitutional to enact a law in this state, enforcing a better observance of the Sabbath?"[333] and "Was the French Revolution of 1793 and the Reign of Bonaparte a benefit to France?"[334] Even the feasibility of "abolishing capital punishment in California" was debated.[335] The Lyceum's home was the Suwanee House (born in January 1852), which boasted a "large bar and dining room."[336] Athletics were enhanced with the birth of the Sacramento Turnverein Gymnastics Society. The Turnverein, whose origins can be traced to nineteenth-century Prussia, not only promoted physical health but also sought to engender social, patriotic and political activity. Sacramentans also could find entertainment and sanctuary with the Sacramento Philharmonic and the Sacramento Musical Society, both of which provided parlor concerts to the general public. Finally, the circus was an undeniable part of early city entertainment. With an association going back to the city's origins, Joseph Rowe's Pioneer Circus was quite the spectacle. An array of horse-riding tricks, tightrope walking, "antipodean feats" and the obligatory clown made Rowe's circus a huge draw.[337]

Despite the extent of the aforementioned legislation, other forms of gambling continued unaffected. Horse racing had been a vibrant feature of Sacramento's gambling culture and was far from being outlawed. As early as 1851, one could wager on bullfights being held in Washington and what would become West Sacramento. By 1854, bull and bear fights were being held, one pitting "a wild California bull and an immense grizzly bear said to weigh 1,600 pounds" against one another.[338] One match, held in April 1856, between bear and bull drew 2,500 people to the city's amphitheater. There was also the allure of dogfights that took place at the corner of Second and K Streets during the summer of 1856. It was reported in the August 15, 1856 *Democratic Journal* that during this period, up to five matches were being held daily.[339] From the odd to the bizarre, wagers were even tendered on dog and badger fights. One organized affair of "badger baiting" came off in December 1858 when John Legget's dog, Leo, took on a badger in an alley between J and K and Front and Second Streets. Spectators were admitted for a sum of fifty cents to see the sad ordeal that lasted ten minutes. The result was a severely mauled Leo, both in the chest and side, with "the badger being apparently uninjured."[310]

Perhaps the most inventive gamble came off in late May 1857, courtesy of Engine Companies No. 1 and 5. The scenario pitted each group's fire engine against the other in a race down M Street, from Twenty-first to Ninth, with the stipulation that the company "that runs the distance in the least time wins the wager."[311] By all indications, this was truly a citywide event; a reported "two or three thousand persons present," most of whom gathered at either the start or finish lines and at the corner of M and Tenth Streets, were greeted with beer wagons and fruit stands. The engines, each weighing more than three thousand pounds, were pulled by a limit of twenty-five company members. When the challenge ended, the Knickerbockers stood victorious with a time of six minutes and fifty-two seconds. The Confidence Boys were barely bested at a time of seven minutes and five seconds. The wager between companies was $250, with no telling how much money changed hands between those in the general public. On a related note, since the summer of 1854, firefighters had had their own saloon, fittingly called the Hydrant. A brief advertisement implored those fond of "fun, fight, or fire" to quench their thirst at the new saloon, located next door to the city's No. 3 Engine House on Third Street between K and L.[312]

Even with the departure of the Arcade and others like it, saloons persisted to be places of violence. Keenan's Fashion suffered a stretch of violence starting in spring 1855. The most disturbing incident took place in early September.[313] The fight appeared typical until the "two of the more enthusiastic individuals" were pried apart and it was found that "the nasal appendage of one" was "being firmly held by the dental organs of the other." Perhaps this was the simple migration of Arcadian ire from one saloon to another, but this had to be far from the kind of Fashion that Keenan envisioned, especially with various physical renovations in play. Regardless, the new Fashion was complete by September, with a new address at 29 J Street. A saloon and billiards room occupied the first floor, while on the second, one would find sleeping apartments. Courtesy of the city's Eureka Foundry, the signature design feature of the new Fashion was an iron façade striking a "unique pattern" of recessed Greco-Roman columns.[314] In June 1856, Keenan ceded half the saloon's control to James "Jimmy" Gunning; by July, Gunning held sole possession of the Fashion. In his late thirties at the time of purchase, the Ohio native guaranteed to "spare no pains to make his Saloon 'THE FASHION' of the city."[315]

Chapter 5
THE EBBING TIDE OF THE GAMBLING SALOON: 1857–60

In January 1857, a curious resident of Sacramento escaped from a saloon on Second Street. "Jocko" the monkey, a trained fixture at an unnamed saloon, broke out and immediately scampered east, where he made his way to the roof of the Western Hotel on Tenth and K. It was there that "he amused himself looking into windows, climbing up and sliding down the awning posts and performing various antics to the infinite amusement of a crowd on the opposite side of the street."[346]

If 1857 came in like a monkey, what would the rest of the year be like? The temperance movement again reorganized and added to its ranks. One addition—the Cold Water Army—was led by the curiously named G.I.N. Monell. The group's ranks were stocked with an energetic and "goodly number of petite specimens of humanity of different ages, sizes, and sexes."[347] The Cold Water Army was reinforced by an anti-swearing society, housed at the corner of J and Eighth Streets. At least in the early going, the society funded itself by assessing monetary penalties to members that swore at five cents a transgression.[348]

Further moral jostling took place during the spring and summer of 1858. As March appeared, the state legislature's ninth session approved an act "for the better observance of the Sabbath," making it a misdemeanor to "[on Sundays] keep open any store, warehouse, mechanic shop, workshop, banking house, manufacturing establishment, or other business house for business purposes."[349] A notable exception, however, related to taverns and restaurants, which the act would "not apply to or in any manner affect."[350]

Accordingly, on the first official day of action, in early June, several saloons—unaware of how the law was to be interpreted—held regular hours. The next day, proprietors Whitemore, Lothamer, Kleibitz & Green, Harris, Cody, Benjamin, Trestler, Hector and Newman were all arrested for violation of what would become known as the Sunday Law.

Justice C.A. Hill's decision to recognize saloons in his interpretation related to (1) saloons being places of business and (2) his thought that "it could not be the intention of the Legislature that keepers of drinking saloons should be allowed to expose for sale and sell their merchandise—cigars, liquors, etc.—when the sale of the same is prohibited at other places."[351]

Coming to the saloon owners' defense was attorney Joseph W. Winans, who believed the law to be unconstitutional. With the law not on the books for even a month, the California Supreme Court agreed, striking the act down. It felt that the legislature was usurping its popularly granted powers and infringing "upon the liberty of the citizen by restraining his right to acquire property."[352]

A lofty term like "liberty" used in reference to the saloon is significant, especially when looking at the social and legal influence of Sacramento's saloon community. Their defiance found organization in 1861 with the formation of the Sacramento Liquor Dealers' Association, which held its first meeting at Stanford's Hall at Third and K. Included were names like Jacob Remmel of the Metropolitan Saloon; Joe Harris of the self-styled Harris's Saloon; the Fashion's John C. Keenan, standing as the group's first president; and W.J. Cady of the Colonnade, its vice-president. Willingness to challenge the Sunday Law's legality was the sole requirement for admission to the group, which went on to nominate and endorse candidates for local and state offices.

It is here that the steady infusion of Germans and other Central, Southern and Eastern Europeans to Sacramento, and its general effect on the city's moral prospectus, holds significance. Simply put, the Germanic-style Sunday of after-church drinking, dancing and general *Gemütlichkeit* ran contrary to the mores of the pious, puritanical sectarians of older American stock who saw Sunday merrymaking as profane. Ironically, the same Americans who sought a dry nation and penitent Sundays were the ones who were both fighting against slavery and promoting equal rights. It's not a stretch to say that the looming Civil War shifted the puritan focus to keeping the Union together and elevating America's former slaves and away from prohibition. Even still, the prohibition movement had not been quashed; rather a slow, droning *Kulturkampf* over alcohol consumption would last well into the next century, accented by the Eighteenth and Twenty-first Amendments.

Anton Miller made the Ohio Brewery go, and his wife made it go after he could not. *Sacramento Public Library.*

Maintaining a Teutonic theme, the late 1850s saw additional names added to Sacramento's list of breweries, the most important being the Ohio Brewery, located between Sixth and Seventh Streets and F and G Streets. Advertisements started to appear for the business in late 1855 but were found with somewhat greater regularity into 1857. The owner of the brewery—previously known as the Union Brewery—was a K. Stuelinger. His sales agent was Anton Miller, a native of Baden, Germany, in his mid-fifties. Also near the beginning of 1857, the Ohio established a saloon much closer to Sacramento's commercial heart on Fifth Street between J and K. Near the end of 1858, the brewery was producing, on average, about five hundred gallons of lager per week.[353]

As Miller soon gained total control over the Ohio, the brewery's operations expanded. He poured some $22,000 into the brewery in 1860. The most salient addition was a 32-foot by 82-foot beer hall "set aside for

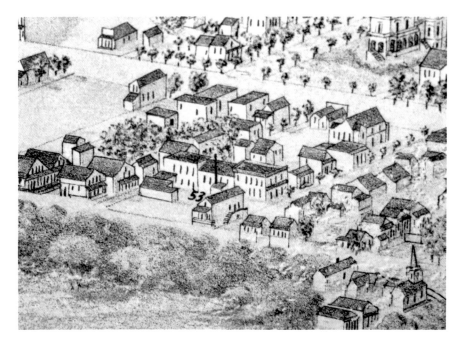

Taken from August Koch's 1870 birds-eye view of Sacramento, the Ohio Brewery sits on the shore of China Slough. *Sacramento Public Library.*

accommodation of Societies or parties who wish to assemble."[351] It also appears that one of the brewery's two cellars—each measuring 30 feet by 50 feet—was refit by Miller to serve as a saloon. The brewery itself was large at 30 feet by 162 feet and three stories in height, making it the largest in the city. It was also large enough for Miller to make his home there.

Also appearing on the scene in 1857 was the Tiger Brewery, located at K and Thirty-first. Originally known as the Franklin Brewery, it was constructed sometime after 1853 by German immigrant Peter Yager. After this time and prior to 1857, it came under the ownership of James Rablin, originally from Cornwall, England, via Illinois, and Robert O. Smith, a native of Wisconsin. It would be their choice to give the brewery the fearsome feline moniker.

Until March 1858, the Tiger produced only lager beer. However, Rablin, Smith and company saw their brewing niche residing in both English and cream ales. Touting its Rablin's Tiger Ale as the "Greatest Beverage of the Season," the brewery was confident enough in its product to "challenge comparison with any Ale made in the state."[355] The *Democratic Journal* corroborated the boast in feeling that the "rich flavor, foaming appearance and cooling qualities recommend it more effectually than anything we can say."[356] By the spring of 1859, the Tiger's lighter ale, also known as "Smith's Sacramento Cream Ale," was "favorably known in different parts of the state."[357] The primary competitor for the cream-ale market was the Bay Area's Albany Brewery. Porter also was coming into production at the Tiger by around the same time. Eventually, because of its rededication to English-style beers, the business would rename itself the English Brewery near the end of the decade.

The Tiger's primary distribution point was Rablin's Exchange, located at the corner of Tenth and K. The Exchange had always possessed the ability to board patrons, especially teamsters who could make use of the business's "hay yard and stables" and fresh water.[358] It also served as a polling place in 1852 for the city's Third Ward.

German contractor Peter Yager built the Franklin Brewery. It would soon take on the moniker of Tiger Brewery. *California State Library.*

As for Keseberg's Phoenix, by 1858, it had started to diversify its production to include more than its signature Lager Beer. The expansion of the brewery would include—like the Columbus—a distillery, which meant the production of malt whiskey "made of the finest quality of Malt, by an experienced Distiller and pronounced by the best judges as equal to the imported Scotch or Irish Whisky."[359] Keseberg went as far as making it possible for potential patrons to sample his products by visiting the brewery or the Lady Adams Co., on K Street between Front and Second.

By midsummer 1858, the city's five lager breweries were going strong, producing some 7,800 gallons of beer per week.[360] While half of this amount was consumed by Sacramento itself, most of the other half was sent to surrounding mines, with a smaller amount being sent to a few cities to the south. The Bay Area remained a largely impenetrable market, as its nineteen breweries were more than enough to keep Sacramento Valley beers from crossing the Carquinez Strait.

Perhaps it was an omen when, in the spring of 1858, William McCall accidentally shot himself in the foot after dropping his gun on the floor of the reading room, but financial woes took their toll on the Orleans, especially after Joseph H Virgo took control of the operation from Hardenbergh.[361] The once seemingly irrepressible Orleans was forced to close in April 1859. In the fall of 1859, a sad epilogue was written to the Orleans saga with word arriving that Count Bidleman was ill. Family members rushed to San Francisco to be by his side, but by November 9, Bidleman had died from what the *Union* described as a "disease of the heart."[362]

We have spoken at length about the heterogeneous nature of Gold Rush Sacramento. One ethnic enclave to feel an acute streak of tragedy as the 1850s droned on was that of the Germans. Initial events centered around the person of Maria Rupp, a twenty-five-year-old beauty from the Hesse region of western Germany and operator of the Sacramento Beer Saloon on K Street between Third and Fourth Streets. Maria had been running the prosperous saloon since January 1856. That would change, however, on the evening of November 18, 1857. Rupp, while playing the saloon's piano, was stabbed in the chest with a butcher knife. She was alert enough to call for a physician but was dead within fifteen minutes.

The killer was a German named Peter Metz. Other than the fact that he was a cook and that his age was between thirty and thirty-five, not much is known of him. He was friendly with Maria, but their relationship was strained by Peter's unrequited affections. Several times, he had asked for her hand in marriage, each time being rebuffed. On the day of the murder, Metz had told John Zwicker, owner of his own saloon on Third Street, that Maria had agreed to marry him. The claim seemed unbelievable to Zwicker, who was chilled over by Metz's ominous comment: "If she did not have him she would not marry anybody else; that she should die first."[363] So convinced was Metz that his romantic fortunes had turned that he ordered an entire bottle of wine and drank "to his marriage and future wife."[364] He also acquired the notion that he would take control of her business on the following day. His last words to Zwicker prior to proceeding to Maria's were simply "that he would go over and see if the business was all right."[365]

A few days later, Maria's funeral service was held at the Saint Rose of Lima Catholic Church on Seventh and K Streets. Beloved as she was, her cortege numbered twenty-three carriages, buggies, etc. Pallbearers wore white scarves and white roses. After a service conducted by the Reverend Father Cassin, her body was transported to the City Cemetery, "where a requiem was sung by a quartette of German vocalists."[306] Maria was gone, and the trial of Peter Metz went on for weeks until he was found guilty of murder in the second degree. He was transported to the state prison at San Quentin, where he would serve out as much of a life sentence as was naturally possible.

The ordeal of Maria's loss, however, was not yet over. After a short stay at San Quentin, Metz's odd behavior was enough to have him transplanted to a "lunatic asylum" near Stockton. Soon after arriving, he escaped, making his way up toward

The headstone of Maria Rupp. As a darling of Sacramento's close-knit German community, her untimely death devastated the lives of many. *Sacramento Public Library.*

Marysville. Although being spotted by several locals, he was able to elude capture. After getting as far north as Siskiyou County, Metz was seized and returned to the Stockton asylum. It was reported in the *Union* that he took the matter "very coolly," contentedly remarking that all of the return travel expenses would cost him nothing.[367]

The next venue for Germanic sadness was the Father Rhine House. Located at 268 J Street between Ninth and Tenth, it was owned by A.J. Bayer, a German from Hannover. His desire to ensure a good time for all of his customers rose to his detriment in the winter of 1857. It was the sentiment of Bayer's immediate neighbor, the Philadelphia House, that the "dancing, music, hilarity and consequent noise" proceeding "long after midnight and the boarders of the Philadelphia House, which stands adjoining, have consequently been much disturbed."[368] It was also the *Union's* contention that Bayer ran the headquarters of "all girls who follow the occupation of street musicians," or what may appear to be antebellum music groupies.[369] The paper went on to say that "dancing went on whether one of these strolling musicians chanced to present or not and that sometimes a white and at other times a black fiddler was engaged."[370] Regardless, the Father Rhine had a reputation that Bayer was seemingly far from disputing or changing, as the Father Rhine's clear mission was to enable the unbridled merrymaking that comes with the German tradition of *Gemütlichkeit*. Accordingly, a few years later, in November 1860, the Father Rhine was up to its old tricks. At eight o'clock in the evening, friends of the proprietor gathered in front of the saloon "armed with tin horns, tin pans, bells, brass kettles, whistles and all uncouth implements that could be thought of for the production of the most horrible noises." Such went on for over an hour, at which time the group dispersed. Again, the *Union* demanded that "enough was enough, even of a good thing."[371]

It was not long before revelry turned to sadness for many of those who knew Bayer and the Father Rhine. On an early spring day in 1861, C.M. Tubbs, a young farmer, found a dead body floating on the Yolo side of the Sacramento River, just south of present-day West Sacramento. It was A.J. Bayer, "lodged among willows near the shore."[372] Reaching his latter forties, the saloonkeeper was survived by a wife and daughter. The backdrop of Bayer's melancholy and resulting suicide resided in the stuff of both tragedy and modern tabloid. Prior to the discovery of his body, Bayer had been missing for more than two weeks. A witness, F. Haug, revealed that Bayer, under heavy intoxication and with tears running down his face, claimed that he would not see his fiftieth birthday. Bayer's downfall came with the seduction and eventual impregnation of a young girl who had been living with his family. The details of the incident were revealed when Bayer was arrested along with his wife and mother for attempting an abortion on the young girl.

In the late summer of 1857, John C. Keenan was back at the Fashion, but he was not alone. His partner this time would be William M. Metzler. However, just days before the reopening, on July 27, near tragedy struck the Keenan family. At their home, near the corner of Fourth and N Streets, Keenan and his wife, Rosana, were readying for bed. As Rosana refilled a camphene-burning lamp, the pouring canister exploded, sending burning liquid all over her. The damage done—burnt breasts, arms and hands— was severe, but a quick-to-the-scene Keenan prevented so much more from happening by covering his wife with a blanket and extinguishing the flames.[373]

Keenan's life then took a few more interesting turns. In May 1858, he boarded the steamer *Eclipse* out of Sacramento, bound for the Fraser River,

One of Sacramento's early renaissance men, John C. Keenan died young of a heart attack while walking the stairs to his San Francisco apartment. *Sacramento Public Library*.

which was experiencing a gold rush of its own. The prospects of the Fraser, located in lower British Columbia, Canada, were enticing enough that he and others were intent on making "a tour of reconnaissance."[371] While abroad, Keenan and his wife adopted three children: James, Jennie and M.J. Perhaps the need for a more steady line of work forced Keenan's brood back to Sacramento. In any case, by June 1860, Keenan and a new co-owner conducted a private reopening of the Fashion.

Also at this time, the Sacramento region was, at last, finding its wine-growing legs. By 1857, the state as a whole had pushed its annual production to a prodigious 246,518 gallons, compared to 58,055 in 1850.[375] Smith's Gardens made its expected contribution. It was Mr. Smith's firm belief "that wine is soon to become the first great staple of California and that our valley, together with the foothills, are particularly adapted to the culture and rapid growth of the grape."[376] In late summer 1860, Smith's arsenal of grape types included the following: Black Hamburg, Black Prince, Black St. Peter's, Grizzly Frontignan, Muscadine Royal and Muscat Cannon Hall. He could also claim the cultivation of roughly 10,500 grapevines.[377]

A.P. Smith's horticultural efforts were set at his gardens two miles east of Sacramento proper along the American River. *Sacramento Public Library.*

Wilson Flint was an early grower of wine grapes in Sacramento, just south of the central city along the Sacramento River. *California State Library.*

Closer to the city center, the Grühler Brothers' vineyard, located on K Street between Fifteenth and Sixteenth, was highly regarded for its "scientifically trimmed" vines and "abundance of fruit."[378] And just south of Sacramento, at the ranch of J.G. Almard, the muscat grape was being grown "much fairer and larger than the Mediterranean grape, esteemed so great a luxury in the east."[379] Also near Almard's was the vineyard of Wilson Flint, where "cultivated on rich alluvial soil" one could find the following varieties of grape: White Muscat of Alexandria, Purple Damascus, Black Zinfandel, Catawba and Black Hamburg.[380]

The first appearance of locally produced wine in a Sacramento saloon was recorded in August 1859. Noted for its "genteel, quiet and comfortable character," the Metropolitan Saloon, on J Street and Third, served a California Red, vintage 1858. It was manufactured by Jacob Knauth, whose vineyards were part of the Sutter Floral Garden, in effect since 1851 and located on the corner of J and Twenty-ninth Streets at Sutter Hall.[381] According to the *Union*, the wine "was pronounced excellent. We hope to see the time when the… prevailing drink will be our native wines and have no doubt that Sacramento County will be able to supply sufficient thereof for home consumption."[382]

With wine flowing, Sacramento's exotic saloon menagerie grew in kind, including a South American anaconda that, in June 1859, escaped from its box.[383] The massive reptile had been on display at a K Street saloon for several days. For roughly a twenty-four-hour period, city residents were on edge with rumors that a child had been swallowed. Such hearsay persisted until a wagon and its frightful—and likely frightened—cargo was found on L Street, where it was captured.

In the mid-1850s, the Mountaineer House drew patrons with "a grey eagle captured on the Sierra Nevada."[384] The bird appears to have been a total spectacle, receiving "the attention and compliments of visitors with becoming dignity." Patrons were able to interact with the bird by feeding it various meats.

The late 1850s also saw new entries into the saloon fraternity. One of the more popular was the Sazerac, owned by native New Yorker John C. Combes and located on the corner of Second and J. The saloon's name refers to what may have been the nation's first mixed drink. Born in New Orleans by druggist/mixologist Monsieur Antoine Peychaud, the Sazerac was a compounded mixture of cognac, sugar and aromatic bitters. As time went on, American rye and whiskey were substituted for Peychaud's French cognac.

An amusing tale of culinary lust came out of the Sazerac in late 1857.[385] Like many saloons, it possessed an oyster bar. The saloon's owner furnished a new employee with a key so as to open the saloon early for preparation. When morning came, the new employee was nowhere to be found and the entire stock of oysters had been consumed. Less the oysters, in the summer of 1858, the Sazerac moved into a new brick building on J Street. We benefit from a detailed description provided by the *Union*. The new saloon covered an area of twenty-eight feet on J Street and fifty feet on Second. It included two aboveground floors, plus a cellar that was seven feet deep. The interior was "elegantly fitted, being elaborately and tastefully painted in fresco, ceiling and walls. Conspicuous in the bar is the sculptured head of a lion, in marble, from the mouth of which several fine jets of water are constantly playing into the marble basin below."[386]

The close collaboration of contractors, so necessary in the construction of a saloon, is illustrated through the Sazerac: architect, M.F. Butler; builder, John Voorhies; mason, Walter Prosser; ornamental painter and designer, William Sefton; painters, Noonen and Co.; marble work, P.T. Devine; and plasterer, W. Mara.

Just months after opening, the Sazerac was hit with violence. The encounter between J.J. Watson and W.H. Taylor started off pleasantly enough.[387] After Taylor threw twenty dollars in gold pieces onto the bar to pay for drinks, Watson countered that such wealth should enable Taylor to pay the money he owed him. After Taylor remarked that the owed sum was only fifteen dollars and that that it had already been repaid, Watson snapped, striking Taylor "about the head and body, breaking the bones of the right leg between the knee and ankle." Once saloon-goers intervened, Taylor was taken to the Orleans House for medical care.

By late 1860, the Sazerac was offering "newspapers from all parts of the state" and had become one of the first saloons to offer a free lunch, served up every morning at eleven o'clock.[388] The free lunch's origins appear to rest, in part, with the advent of commercial drugs and their impressive physiological effects, often matching or surpassing those of alcohol. The Saint George Drug Store at Fourth and J, R.H. McDonald and Company at 139 J and Redington and Company in San Francisco offered an assortment of elixirs—Davis' Pain Killer, Baker's Pain Panacea and Moffat's Bitters were just a few. It's not known how much alcohol content actually resided in the aforesaid "medications," but some, like the "locally produced Marvelous Remedy for Man and Beast," could be composed of as much as 70 percent alcohol. Such a robust alternative to liquor portended a potential loss of market share for the city's saloons. The salooning community's counterpoint was the enticement of free food, which, of course, wasn't completely free. In return for a meal, patrons were expected to purchase a minimum number of drinks. Without compliance, someone tantamount to the modern-day "bouncer" would remove the freeloader, which meant that bartenders, like in any other era, were not selected for their weak frame but for brawn.[389]

For those already accustomed to paying for a daily drink or two, what would come to be known as the "free lunch" proved a boon. One of the first Sacramento saloons to offer the free lunch was the Pearl. Operated by Charles Voigt and located on Third Street, it was called a "beautiful and neatly furnished saloon" by the *Democratic Journal*.[390] Established in the spring of 1853, it was originally known as the Eastman, named for its first owner, W.A. Eastman. By July, however, the catchier Pearl moniker was applied. The saloon's advertisement in the 1854–55 *City Directory* tempted readers with free portions of oyster, chicken and gumbo soup.

The free lunch's reign was a long but not indefinite one. While 1919's Volstead Act may have devastated the alcoholic punch of Western saloons, it killed the free lunch. And although repeal had a somewhat rehabilitating effect on the saloon industry, it clearly was not the same place that it used to be. The free lunch became an amusing footnote of history and went on to be nothing more than a convenient little idiom. Moreover, today's peanuts and occasional bowl of crackers are a far cry from the nineteenth-century saloon's impressive selection of smoked oysters, cold cuts and terrapin soup, the last offering a common free lunch sight at Keenan's Fashion.

Chapter 6
LAST CALL: 1861

News of the Confederacy's April 12, 1861 shelling of Fort Sumter did not immediately reach Sacramento. When it did so, on April 24, it was clear that Civil War Sacramento was, almost exclusively, a city standing on the Union side. In August, the *Union*, based on a view of the city from an elevated point, remarked at how "the heart of our community is right on the great question of the Union. There was not one flag less afloat from our flagstaffs on account of the late disaster in Virginia[391] but the folds of the national banner in all its beauty floated calmly over the city. We have conclusive evidence of the true and earnest patriotism of our citizens."[392]

There was even the establishment of a Union Club that sought, on behalf of the national government, to organize the might of loyal citizens into a group for political and social action. Within a week, the club was able to recruit some one thousand members in Sacramento, and after a month, several chapters had been established throughout Northern California.[393] The city even formed a Union Club for local juveniles.

However, as we well know, the Gold Rush drew hordes of adventurers from the American South to Sacramento, where many chose to stay. While Californians of Northern origin numbered seventy-four thousand in 1860, there were twenty-nine thousand who came from the South.[394] This factor did just enough to engender fear, sometimes panic, in the Union-partial city. Only days after Sumter, when rumors started circulating about a fifth column of Rebel supporters, nervous members of the media claimed "that the Union Club [was] matched at last."[395] A Secessionist flag was seen flying over Forest Hill, along the Truckee Pass, while there was also talk of Rebel sympathizers wearing thoughtfully placed green ribbons for subtle identification. Pockets of Secessionist support were also reported to have existed in Volcano (located in Amador County), as well as at McConnell's Station near present-day Elk Grove. And in August, Unionists listened intently for a rumored salute to be fired off by Secessionists, honoring the Rebel army's July victory at Manassas (First Bull Run).

The salute, however, never came, and although the overall Secessionist presence seemed scattered, disorganized and generally ineffectual, there were moments of sectional confrontation. One of the more heated took place on, of all days, July 4, 1861, when Major J.P. Gillis, a defiant Secessionist and ex-alderman, took on Sacramento's Unionists.[396] Things started with the major's gamey choice to walk about the city with a non-Union flag. When Unionist J.W. Bideman noticed the curious tricolor, he exclaimed to his colleague Curtis Clark, "I'll bet ten dollars that that is a secession flag, and if it is I'm bound to take it if it is unfolded." Sure enough, when Gillis unfolded the flag, it was a Confederate replica of the official first national flag of the Secessionist states. It was then Gillis's choice to march back and forth in front of the St. George Hotel—that is, until Bideman approached Gillis, grabbed him by the throat and tore the flag from his cane. Just moments later, things deteriorated into a childish game of keep-away as Unionists Frank Rhodes from Pennsylvania and A. Burns of Illinois challenged a small group of Secessionists "to come and take it." Not one of the Rebels complied.

The Unionists were keen on showcasing their newly won souvenir, which they did first at Rhodes's own saloon, the Adriatic, located inside the St. George Hotel on Third Street between I and J. The standard, two feet wide and four feet long, was made of silk and featured three stripes—two red and one white—"and on the blue field were ten stars."[397] When it was waved about, one of the stars fell to the ground, causing the revelers to claim that it represented South Carolina, the first state to secede from the Union. When the scorned Gillis learned of the flag's location, he staggered into the Adriatic, pleading for its return. When Rhodes refused, Gillis responded, "Well, sir, I shall be compelled to take it then." But upon making his way around the bar counter, Gillis was restrained, and apparently realizing the futility of the matter, the Southerner relented.

Gillis may have been done, but later that day, Secessionists were brazen enough to also remove a Union flag from the city's Masonic Hall. That same day went on to be marred with the occurrence of several fights "at the Orleans and the Union Hotels; pistols were drawn at [Keenan's] Fashion

Saloon…on the secession question and several fights came off at the Champion Saloon," owned by Irishman E. Lloyd and located at the corner of Second and K.[398]

While the Fourth of July was a clear lightning rod for sectional anger, the earliest recorded Yankee-Rebel saloon confrontation looks to have taken place in the early days of May at the Bank Exchange. Contact between H. Derrick, a Unionist, and T. Calloway, a Secessionist, deteriorated to the point where one challenged the other to a duel.[399] They both agreed to do so early the next morning at seven o'clock. However, when neither man showed, many wondered what impact the previous evening's excesses may have had. Later that day, they reconnected and decided to again meet for a duel in the coming hours. But when Derrick showed and Calloway did not, much of the tension leading up to the duel was defused. During the evening, both men met and discussed their differences amicably, "and the parties having been friends formerly became friends again."

If only on a modest scale, the operations of one local brewery were also affected by the war. Soon after the start of hostilities, a Union army installation, the aptly named Camp Union, was established just south of Sacramento City limits near present-day Sutterville Road and William Land Park. Due to inadequate accommodations, the installation was removed from its original location, that being on the Yolo side of the Sacramento River. Once finding a final home, the camp was officially christened in early October 1861 when its commander, Major Coult, smashed a bottle of California red wine against the camp flagstaff.

Also setting up in the Sutterville area was the newly founded Sutterville Brewery. The business was under the ownership of Martin Arenz, a thirty-one-year-old Prussian who had operated two saloons prior to going into the brewing business, the Indian Queen Saloon on 56 Third Street and, before that, the Central Saloon on J between Fifth and Sixth. The structure containing the brewery—the Vance Building, named for its original occupant—was constructed in 1853 as a grocery store, but with visions of a bustling Sutterville never materializing, it was soon vacated. That is, until the beginning of the decade, when Arenz purchased the three-story brick building (including a basement) for $1,500.[100]

With less than a quarter mile separating Arenz's Sutterville Brewery from Camp Union, the chance of contact between the two neighbors was inevitable. It came during the Christmas season of 1861, when a dozen or so intoxicated soldiers from the camp made their way to the brewery, demanding refreshments.[101] When the brewery workers refused, the soldiers

A view of the Sutterville Brewery in 1906. *California State Library.*

"started to break things," and a large fight quickly ensued. The brewers stood pat, retaliating with brickbats and driving off a bulk of the soldiers. Arenz was brazen enough to fire a pistol at the attackers, although missing. Thankfully, just as the bluecoats attempted to return, a detachment of fellow recruits from Camp Union intervened, ending the fight and saving both sides from a potential disaster.

By the early days of the Civil War, Sacramento City had just passed its tenth birthday. Concurrently, the city's saloon community had reached a well-earned degree of maturity and was able to claim a heritage so closely tied to the biggest rush for riches the world had ever seen. The viability of the saloon proved slippery, however, begging the question of how many of those established during the time of the city's incorporation—or even at the start of the Gold Rush—were still around at the end of the decade. Perhaps coming as a surprise, few, if any, could claim as to have done as much. If a quick comparison of directory listings for saloons from 1853 and 1861 reveals nearly 100 percent turnover, we can honestly conclude that for saloon operators, long-term business prospects were frail at best.

Part and parcel to this, we see an industry in a state of constant regeneration. Losing a few members here but adding others there, the saloon community grew like a chameleon that, although not changing size, was often to change its look and identity. If natural hazards to the saloon—fire, flood and even disease—were difficult enough to overcome, the competition in the saloon industry could be unforgivable. By decade's end, if one hundred saloons were serving some ten thousand Sacramentans, there would have been a ratio of one saloon for every one hundred residents. The economies of scale in this scenario were not favorable to most of those in the business, with the result being frequent turnover. In a more positive light, the hazardous business environment, not to mention Adam Smith's invisible hand, guaranteed the patronizing community a near-constant dynamism and freshness in their choice of establishments.

As mentioned earlier, the ability to attract patrons via some hook was a clear difference-maker in a saloon's livelihood, and the hunt for viable entertainment must have been an enormous challenge. If this weren't enough, there were additional hurdles relative to the costs of alcohol acquisition. Whether a saloon chose to acquire its product through a wholesaler or directly from a brewery or distillery, the costs could be high, although one would believe that the diversity of breweries had a stabilizing effect on the overall price of beer. Even so, if a particular saloon could not draw patrons, the looming factor of overhead could kill a business. This didn't include the prohibitive cost that came with the licensing of gambling accommodations and the right to sell liquor. The aggregate of these variables wielded a much greater degree of peril over the life of the saloon than that of any temperance group.

A paramount factor in a saloon's survival relates to the character of the person who ran the place. Keenan, Johnson, Daly and Gibson all operated establishments that lasted. Their dynamism—in the extracurricular realms of politics, firefighting, prospecting, paramilitarism, cooking and franchising—set them apart. Pursuing such varied interests took effort, an effort so easily transferable to the everyday piloting of a saloon's operations. It is more than believable that dabbling in so many arenas created connections, relationships of business, politics and overall good will that fed the attractiveness of their establishments time and time again. Who they were and what they were willing to do to promote their spots proved distinguishing, yielding them the commercial longevity that every saloon owner so desired.

Regardless of their early economic outlook, by the dawn of the 1860s, saloons and their cultural offerings were firmly entrenched within the Sacramento ethos. Just ahead were four more years of bloody civil war, enough flooding to rechannel where the American River met the Sacramento (not to mention the raising of the central business district) and the establishment of a transcontinental railroad. The advent of rail, first in 1855 and then in 1863, was a clear boon for the saloon. It increased Sacramento's community of unskilled labor overnight, thus filling any vacuum created by the departure of miners. The region's agriculture prowess, which came into its own in the 1880s, also guaranteed that thousands of parched field workers and hands would eventually belly up to the bar. Through it all, the institution flourished, and for decades to come, perhaps with not as much verve as it did prior to the Civil War, Sacramento's saloons would carry forth a legacy and a story worthy of telling so long after bidding adieu to history.

It should be noted that the saloon's impact on Sacramento's social identity was remarkable. Where the spirit of equality seems to have failed so miserably in the mining camps, the saloon conducted and primed at least some element of racial and ethnic mixing. It was a hothouse for the distillation of political views, ideas and the compelling issues of the day. In an environment that placed a premium on the male mystique, it was also an arena for gender proving. It was the marketplace for brewery, distillery and winery alike; it was a bellwether for the state's moral development, and it even tested the mettle of early crime enforcement.

If nothing else, the antebellum saloon was a prime conductor for violence. The factors of both gaming and drink often elicited a patron's most unpleasant behaviors, and for those already apt to be violent, the saloon's offerings merely worsened their state. Match this with an already beleaguered police force, and the problem further exacerbates. The stories of horrific violence that we've covered are testament to the brutality of antebellum America. Sacramento could even claim to be home to the "Fighting Corner," essentially the intersection of K and Front Streets. The spot developed a deserving reputation in the mid-1850s as a fully hands-on experience, or as one paper wrote, a hotbed of "rowdyism and pugilistic encounters." However, as the Gold Rush waned and California's civic institutions stiffened, saloon violence and related spots of violence like the "Corner" seemed to lose social traction. What's more, as the nation stretched its industrial legs and Sacramento settled into its place as a railroad and agricultural linchpin, the saloon became less a place of succor and curiosity for adventurer, miner and gambler and more a hub for a new breed of California laborer.

NOTES

Chapter 1

1. Hume, "Eagle Theater," 169.
2. Erdoes, *Saloons*, 11.
3. Morse, *First History*, 31.
4. Erdoes, *Saloons*, 9.
5. "Swimming Bath," *Daily Democratic State Journal*, June 15, 1854.
6. "Public Meeting," *Placer Times*, September 22, 1849.
7. Morse, *First History*, 32.
8. Ibid., 33.
9. Decker, *Diaries*, 155.
10. Eifler, *Gold Rush Capitalists*, 159.
11. Erdoes, *Saloons*, 159.
12. Ibid.
13. Morse, *First History*, 32.
14. West, "The Saloon," 14.
15. Ibid, 15.
16. Culver, *Sacramento City Directory*, 79.
17. "A New Species of Drunkenness," *Sacramento Transcript*, December 17, 1850.
18. "Temperance Meeting," *Sacramento Transcript*, June 6, 1850.
19. "Temperance Test in California," *Placer Times*, March 2, 1850.
20. "Siamese Watermelon," *Daily Democratic State Journal*, September 5, 1854.
21. Ibid.
22. "English Ale and Malt Whiskey," *Sacramento Daily Union*, July 29, 1858.
23. "Gold! Gold! Gold!" *Placer Times*, August 11, 1849.

24. Childress, "From Wet to Dry."
25. Census Office, *7ᵗʰ Census, 1850* (Washington, D.C.: Robert Armstrong, Public Printer, 1853), 968–69, 972.

Chapter 2

26. Hume, "Eagle Theater," 171.
27. Morse, *First History*, 32.
28. Ibid., 31.
29. Johnston, *Experiences*, 248.
30. Grimshaw, *Grimshaw's Narrative*, 16.
31. Wright, *History of Sacramento County*, 46.
32. Ibid.
33. Collins, *Sutter's Fort*, 36.
34. Lienhard, *A Pioneer*, 198.
35. Sacramento Probate Court, "Estate of Peter Slater."
36. de Rutte, *Adventures of a Young Swiss*, 16.
37. Lienhard, *A Pioneer*, 75.
38. Olson, *Archeological Investigations*, 14.
39. Schoonover, *Life and Times*, 37.
40. "Brewery," *Placer Times*, February 16, 1850.
41. It is entirely unclear where the title "Galena" comes from.
42. Sacramento Bee, *Sacramento Guide Book*, 51.
43. "A Glass of Lager," *Sacramento Daily Union*, July 20, 1858.
44. Census Office, *7ᵗʰ Census, 1850*, 202–03; Census Office, *8ᵗʰ Census, 1860*, 10–13.
45. "Liquid Manufacturers," *Sacramento Daily Union*, January 2, 1859.
46. Hayes, *Lower American River*, 89–90.
47. "The Plague of Locusts at Smith's Gardens," *Daily Democratic State Journal*, August 5, 1855.
48. Census Office, *7ᵗʰ Census, 1850*.
49. Culver, *Sacramento City Directory*, 226.
50. "United States Brewery," *Sacramento Daily Union*, August 11, 1851.
51. "Grape Cuttings!! Grape Cuttings!!" *Sacramento Daily Union*, March 19, 1851.
52. "Grapes," *Sacramento Transcript*, October 3, 1851.
53. "Foreign vs. Home Wines," *Sacramento Daily Union*, December 16, 1853.
54. Canfield, *Diary*, 31.
55. Taylor, *Eldorado*, 205–06.
56. Ibid.
57. Morse, *First History*, 31.

58. DeArment, *Knights*, 282.
59. Johnston, *Experiences*, 250.
60. Morse, *First History*, 32.
61. Johnston, *Experiences*, 250.
62. Ibid.
63. Ibid, 251.
64. Holladay, *World Rushed In*, 321.
65. "Concerts," *Placer Times*, October 27, 1849.
66. Ryan, *Personal Adventures*, 164–65.
67. Kirker, "El Dorado Gothic," 39.
68. Ibid., 193.
69. Ibid.
70. Hume, "Eagle Theater," 338.
71. Ibid.
72. "Eagle Theater," *Placer Times*, November 7, 1849.
73. Sacramento Court of First Magistrate, *Jones, Brown et all v. Z. Hubbard, Brown and Company*.
74. Ibid.
75. Ibid., *J. Brown v. Hubbard, Brown and Company*.
76. Ibid., *Jones and Brown v. Z. Hubbard, Brown and Company*.
77. "Old Round Tent," *Sacramento Transcript*, August 13, 1850.
78. Hume, "Eagle Theater," 189.
79. Johnston, *Experiences*, 249.
80. Wells and Peterson, *The '49ers*, 152.
81. "The Citizens of Our City," *Sacramento Transcript*, February 12, 1851.
82. "Re-Opening of Hubbard's Exchange," *Sacramento Transcript*, July 6, 1850.
83. Wells and Peterson, *The '49ers*, 195.
84. Wyman, "Sacramento Booms," 165.
85. Bancroft, *History*, 449.
86. Taylor, *Eldorado*, 167.
87. "Our City," *Placer Times*, July 20, 1849.

CHAPTER 3

88. "Early Gaming of California," *San Francisco Morning Call*, May 28, 1893.
89. Brannan, *Scoundrel's Tale*, 307.
90. Ibid., 364.
91. "Mad Dog," *Sacramento Transcript*, June 21, 1850.
92. "Case of Shooting," *Sacramento Transcript*, August 5, 1850.

93. "Proceedings Before the Committee of Investigation," *Sacramento Transcript*, February 26, 1851; "Immense Excitement! Lynch Law at Last," *Sacramento Transcript*, February 26, 1851.

94. Ibid.

95. Ibid.

96. "Funeral of Mr. Myers," *Sacramento Transcript*, February 28, 1851.

97. "Proceedings Before the Committee of Investigation," *Sacramento Transcript*, February 26, 1851; "Immense Excitement! Lynch Law at Last," *Sacramento Transcript*, February 26, 1851.

98. "Immense Excitement! Lynch Law at Last," *Sacramento Transcript*, February 26, 1851.

99. Ibid.

100. Ibid.

101. Ibid.

102. Massey, "A Frenchman in the Gold Rush," 51.

103. "Crime," *Sacramento Transcript*, January 14, 1851.

104. Ibid.

105. *Sacramento Transcript*, March 1, March 3, March 7 and March 10, 1851.

106. Johnson, "Vigilance and the Law," 561.

107. Ibid.

108. Lord, *At the Extremity of Civilization*, 297.

109. Bell, *Reminiscences*, 452.

110. "Empire Saloon," *Sacramento Transcript*, June 26, 1850.

111. Census Office, *7ᵗʰ Census, 1850*.

112. "The Tyrolese Singers," *Sacramento Transcript*, December 6, 1850.

113. "Our Saloons," *Sacramento Transcript*, February 15, 1851.

114. "Music for the Crowd," *Sacramento Transcript*, September 21, 1850.

115. Lord, *At the Extremity of Civilization*, 297.

116. "The Musicians of the City," *Sacramento Transcript*, August 29, 1850.

117. Gerstäcker, *California Gold Mines*, 42.

118. "Music," *Sacramento Transcript*, September 24, 1850.

119. "A New Feature," *Sacramento Transcript*, October 11, 1850.

120. Howe, *Argonauts*, 156.

121. "The Orleans and the El Dorado," *Sacramento Transcript*, October 28, 1850.

122. "The Orleans House," *Sacramento Transcript*, December 3, 1850.

123. Lord, *At the Extremity of Civilization*, 306.

124. Simpson, "Sacramento's Historic Buildings," 5.

125. "Still Another Shooting Affray," *Sacramento Daily Union*, November 4, 1852.

126. "Early Gaming of California," *San Francisco Morning Call*, May 28, 1893.

127. "Lee's Exchange," *Sacramento Transcript*, June 26, 1850.

128. "Empire Saloon," *Sacramento Transcript*, June 26, 1850.

129. Lord, *At the Extremity of Civilization*, 284.

130. Ibid.

131. "Early Gaming of California," *San Francisco Morning Call*, May 28, 1893.

132. Davis, "Research Use of County Court Records," 244.

133. Ibid.

134. "An Affray," *Sacramento Transcript*, February 24, 1851.

135. Secrest, *Blood and Honor*, 6.

136. "Dueling," *Sacramento Daily Union*, August 10, 1852.

137. "Sparring To-night," *Sacramento Transcript*, June 15, 1850.

138. "American Saloons," *Sacramento Daily Union*, February 18, 1852.

139. "The Orleans and the El Dorado," *Sacramento Transcript*, October 28, 1851.

140. Lord, *At the Extremity of Civilization*, 306.

141. "The 'El Dorado' in Sacramento," *Illustrated London News*, June 5, 1852.

142. "Early Gaming of California," *San Francisco Morning Call*, May 28, 1893.

143. Ibid.

144. "Daring Outrage," *Sacramento Daily Union*, June 7, 1851.

145. *Sacramento Daily Union*, Crime Reports for 1853 and 1859.

146. "Police—Health," *Sacramento Daily Union*, June 3, 1854.

147. "Our Police," *Daily Democratic State Journal*, October 8, 1853.

148. "A Man Shot," *Sacramento Daily Union*, December 18, 1851.

149. "Fatal Affray," *Sacramento Daily Union*, June 3, 1852.

150. Ibid.

151. "Shooting Affray," *Sacramento Daily Union*, October 27, 1852.

152. "Musical Row," *Sacramento Daily Union*, December 18, 1851.

153. "Renovating," *Sacramento Transcript*, March 10, 1851.

154. Bell, *Reminiscences*, 451.

155. "City Affairs," *Sacramento Transcript*, September 8, 1850.

156. "An Assault," *Sacramento Transcript*, October 15, 1850.

157. Bell, *Reminiscences*, 373.

158. "Humboldt Furniture for Sale," *Sacramento Transcript*, May 1851.

159. "The Oriental Saloon," *Sacramento Daily Union*, July 28, 1851.

160. "Oriental Saloon," *Sacramento Daily Union*, July 17, 1851.

161. "The Bloomer of Fashion," *Sacramento Daily Union*, July 15, 1851.

162. Tinling, "Bloomerism Comes to California," 21.

163. Bosker, *Bowled Over*, 16.

164. "The Oriental" *Sacramento Daily Union*, July 4, 1851.

165. Lord, *At the Extremity of Civilization*, 297.

166. "Opening of the Oregon," *Sacramento Transcript*, August 23, 1850.

167. "A New Feature," *Sacramento Transcript*, October 11, 1850.

168. "Opening of the Oregon," *Sacramento Transcript*, August 23, 1850.

169. de Rutte, *Adventures of a Young Swiss*, 74.

170. Lapp, "Negro in Gold Rush California," 88.

171. Borthwick, *Gold Hunters*, 135.

172. Johnston, *Experiences*, 563.

173. "Influx of Frenchmen," *Sacramento Daily Union*, July 1852; "Another Murderous Assault," *Sacramento Daily Union*, November 10, 1851.

174. "Man Shot," *Sacramento Daily Union*, April 7, 1852.

175. "Fatal Affray," *Sacramento Daily Union*, July 5, 1852.

176. "William Green," *Daily Democratic State Journal*, October 18, 1853.

177. "A Failure," *Daily Democratic State Journal*, December 19, 1853.

178. "The Magnolia," *Sacramento Daily Union*, April 21, 1851.

179. "The Magnolia," *Sacramento Daily Union*, June 20, 1851.

180. "Death of a Pioneer Citizen," *Sacramento Bee*, April 23, 1877.

181. "The Magnolia," *Sacramento Daily Union*, December 3, 1851.

182. Wright, *History of Sacramento County*, 152.

183. Ibid.

184. "Indian Queen," *Sacramento Daily Union*, January 1, 1853.

185. "Joaquin's Head," *Sacramento Daily Union*, September 6, 1853.

186. "Radford's Saloon," *Sacramento Daily Union*, December 30, 1851.

187. Ibid.

188. Ibid.

189. "Oysters," *Sacramento Daily Union*, March 1, 1852.

190. "Gonorrhea Mixture" and "Syphilis Cured," *California Statesman*, November 22, 1854.

191. "Fanny Seymour, alias Smith," *Sacramento Daily Union*, December 23, 1852.

192. Ibid.

193. "A Man Shot! Great Excitement in Consequence!" *Sacramento Daily Union*, December 21, 1852.

194. "Great Sale Today at the Bull's Head," *Sacramento Daily Union*, April 25, 1851.

195. "The Horse Market," *Sacramento Daily Union*, March 20, 1851.

196. "What's a Free and Easy?" *Sacramento Transcript*, August 1, 1850.

197. "A 'Slice' from the Horse Market," *Sacramento Daily Union*, March 15, 1851.

198. "Melancholy Accident," *Sacramento Transcript*, April 1, 1850.

199. "Died," *Sacramento Daily Union*, December 20, 1854.

200. "Sudden Death," *Sacramento Daily Union*, April 14, 1851.

201. "A New Restaurant," *Sacramento Daily Union*, October 30, 1851.

202. "Re-Opening of the Woodcock," *Sacramento Daily Union*, April 7, 1851.

203. "Burglary," *Sacramento Daily Union*, June 11, 1851.

204. "Robbery," *Sacramento Daily Union*, June 20, 1851.

205. Leach, *Recollections*, 4.

206. Ibid.

207. Ibid.

208. "Awful Conflagration," *Sacramento Daily Union*, November 4, 1852.

209. Ibid.

210. "Incidents of the Fire," *Sacramento Daily Union*, November 4, 1852.

211. "Another Victim," *Sacramento Daily Union*, November 7, 1852.

212. "Incidents of the Fire," *Sacramento Daily Union*, November 4, 1852.

CHAPTER 4

213. Holden, *Sacramento*, 178.

214. "The Bricklayers," *Sacramento Daily Union*, September 27, 1853.

215. "New Brick Building," *Sacramento Daily Union*, November 20, 1852.

216. "Floods in Sacramento," *New York Daily Times*, January 29, 1853.

217. "Orleans Hotel," *Sacramento Daily Union*, January 1, 1853.

218. "The Arrangements," *Daily Democratic State Journal*, January 3, 1853.

219. "The Orleans," *Sacramento Daily Union*, January 1853.

220. "The Arrangements," *Daily Democratic State Journal*, January 3, 1853.

221. "Miska Hauser's Concert," *Sacramento Daily Union*, March 11, 1853.

222. "The Serenaders," *Sacramento Daily Union*, March 12, 1853.

223. "Lola Montez and Her Concert," *Sacramento Daily Union*, July 7, 1853; "All Was Not Sweetness and Gold Dust—They Once Threw Eggs at Lola," *Sacramento Bee*, August 5, 1957.

224. "All Was Not Sweetness and Gold Dust—They Once Threw Eggs at Lola," *Sacramento Bee*, August 5, 1957.

225. "Evening Pastimes," *Sacramento Daily Union*, August 3, 1853.

226. "Soiree Pugilistique," *Sacramento Daily Union*, April 13, 1852.

227. "Ratification Meeting at the Orleans," *Sacramento Daily Union*, April 3, 1853.

228. "New Englanders Attention!" *Sacramento Daily Union*, December 16, 1853.

229. "Beaver Lunch," *Daily Democratic State Journal*, January 1, 1855.

230. "Orleans Hotel," *Sacramento Daily Union*, June 29, 1853.

231. "Turtle Soup," *Sacramento Daily Union*, November 7, 1853.

232. "Billiard Saloon, K Street," *Placer Times*, September 29, 1849.

233. "Sacramento Billiard Factory," *Daily Democratic State Journal*, November 5, 1855.

234. "Fountain," *Daily Democratic State Journal*, July 18, 1854

235. "Worse Than Winning an Elephant," *Daily Democratic State Journal*, July 20, 1856.

236. "Orleans Hotel," *Daily Democratic State Journal*, September 9, 1854; "The Orleans Renovated," *Daily Democratic State Journal*, September 22, 1854.

237. "The Political Hive," *Daily Democratic State Journal*, January 8, 1856.

238. "Shooting Affray," *Sacramento Daily Union*, April 28, 1853.

239. "Early Gaming of California," *San Francisco Morning Call*, May 28, 1893.

240. "Mizzled," *Sacramento Daily Union*, May 24, 1853.

241. "Robbery at the El Dorado," *Sacramento Daily Union*, May 11, 1853.

242. "The Magnolia," *Daily Democratic State Journal*, September 21, 1853.

243. "Conviviality," *Sacramento Daily Union*, August 6, 1853.

244. "Another Fine Building," *Sacramento Daily Union*, July 8, 1853; "The Magnolia," *Daily Democratic State Journal*, September 21, 1853.

245. "The Magnolia," *Daily Democratic State Journal*, September 21, 1853.

246. Ibid.

247. "Free Blow," *Daily Democratic State Journal*, April 20, 1854.

248. "Merchants' Exchange Saloon," *Daily Democratic State Journal*, March 10, 1854.

249. "Foot Racing," *Daily Democratic State Journal*, June 16, 1854.

250. "A Blow Out," *Daily Democratic State Journal*, September 3, 1854.

251. "Know Nothings and Freedom's Phalanx Attend!" *Daily Democratic State Journal*, October 27, 1854.

252. "Mark the Changes of the Fashion," *Sacramento Daily Union*, June 7, 1853.

253. "Sudden Death of Mr. John C. Keenan," *California Alta*, May 26, 1869.

254. Hall, *Old Sacramento*, 66.

255. "The Fashion Saloon, 39 J Street," *Daily Democratic State Journal*, April 17, 1854.

256. "Sutter Race Course," *Daily Democratic State Journal*, May 10, 1854.

257. "The Turf," *Daily Democratic State Journal*, October 20, 1855.

258. Ibid.

259. "Brighton Race Course," *Sacramento Daily Union*, February 7, 1852.

260. "California Barley," *Sacramento Daily Union*, May 11, 1852

261. "Alhambra Saloon," *Daily Democratic State Journal*, December 26, 1852.

262. Ibid.

263. "The Alhambra," *Daily Democratic State Journal*, June 21, 1853.

264. "For Sale," *Sacramento Daily Union*, July 13, 1853.

265. "The Capital Saloon," *Sacramento Daily Union*, April 1, 1854,

266. "Oysters! Oysters!" *California Statesman*, November 21, 1854.

267. Sacramento Genealogical Society, *Women Proprietors*.

268. "The Eagle Exchange," *Sacramento Daily Union*, August 3, 1851.

269. Wright, "Making of Cosmopolitan California, Part II," 73.

270. "Orleans Hotel," *Sacramento Daily Union*, January 21, 1854.

271. "Extra-Ordinary," *Sacramento Daily Union*, September 10, 1852.

272. "Shooting Affair," *Sacramento Daily Union*, September 15, 1861.

273. Boessenecker, *Gold Dust*, 134–35.

274. "Turnbull's Saloon, *Daily Democratic State Journal*, June 1, 1853.

275. "Marion," *Sacramento Daily Union*, March 17, 1853.

276. "Shooting Affair," *Sacramento Daily Union*, April 13, 1854.

277. "Serious Affray," *Sacramento Daily Union*, August 16, 1852.

278. "The Wonder of the World," *Daily Democratic State Journal*, April 13, 1855.

279. "Arcadian Row," *Daily Democratic State Journal*, January 13, 1855.

280. "Row in the Arcade," *Daily Democratic State Journal*, January 18, 1855.

281. "Another Arcadian Row," *Daily Democratic State Journal*, January 25, 1855.
282. "Rows," *Daily Democratic State Journal*, February 14, 1855.
283. "Got the Worst of a Bad Bargain," *California Statesman*, January 20, 1855.
284. "Horrible," *Daily Democratic State Journal*, November 6, 1854.
285. "Lager Beer," *Daily Democratic State Journal*, July 28, 1854.
286. Thrapp, *Encyclopedia of Frontier Biography*, 775–76.
287. Lienhard, *A Pioneer*, 170.
288. Ibid.
289. Ibid., 775.
290. "A Glass of Lager," *Sacramento Daily Union*, July 20, 1858.
291. "Brown's Lager Beer and Chop Saloon," *Daily Democratic State Journal*, May 1, 1855.
292. "Sacramento Beer Cellar," *Daily Democratic State Journal*, July 28, 1854.
293. "Lager Beer," *Daily Democratic State Journal*, August 15, 1854.
294. "Lager Beer," *Daily Democratic State Journal*, December 7, 1854.
295. Colville, *Sacramento City Directory*, xix.
296. "Lager Beer on Ice," *Sacramento Bee*, June 3, 1859.
297. "Sitka Ice House," *Daily Democratic State Journal*, November 16, 1853.
298. Colville, *Colville's Sacramento Directory*, xix.
299. "A Glass of Lager Beer," *Sacramento Daily Union*, July 20, 1858.
300. "Statistics," *Sacramento Daily Union*, August 6, 1853; "Bar Licenses," *Sacramento Transcript*, February 16, 1851.
301. "McWilliams & Co.," *Daily Democratic State Journal*, November 23, 1853; "McWilliams & Co.," *Daily Democratic State Journal*, December 2, 1852.
302. "Drinking Saloons," *Sacramento Daily Union*, November 13, 1852.
303. "Temperance Festival," *Sacramento Daily Union*, December 29, 1853; "The Temperance Festival," *Sacramento Daily Union*, December 30, 1853.
304. "Old Joe," *California Statesman*, February 7, 1855.
305. California State Legislature, "An Act to Take the Sense of the People of This State…," 240.
306. "Prohibitory Liquor Law," *Daily Democratic State Journal*, September 13, 1855.
307. "Beauties of the Maine Liquor Law," *Sacramento Daily Union*, October 3, 1853.
308. "Torch Light Procession," *Daily Democratic State Journal*, October 1855.
309. California State Legislature, "An Act to Prohibit the Collection…," 193.
310. "Liquor Laws," *Sacramento Daily Union*, April 15, 1858.
311. California State Legislature, "An Act to License Gaming," 165–66; "An Act to License Gaming," *Sacramento Transcript*, March 13, 1851.
312. "Gambling on Sunday," *Sacramento Daily Union*, August 7, 1852.
313. California State Legislature, "An Act to Suppress Gaming," 124–25.
314. Ibid.

315. "Melancholy Suicide," *Daily Democratic State Journal*, May 6, 1855.

316. "California Immigration," *Sacramento Transcript*, November 25, 1850.

317. Loosely, "Foreign Born Population of California," 5.

318. Ibid.

319. Hamilton, "Adventurism and the California Gold Rush," 1,469.

320. Wright, "Making of Cosmopolitan California, Part I," 341.

321. Findlay, *People of Chance*, 95.

322. Ibid., 99.

323. "The Issue," *Daily Democratic State Journal*, May 21, 1856.

324. "Law—Order—The Action of the People in San Francisco," *Sacramento Daily Union*, May 21, 1856.

325. Findlay, *People of Chance*, 99.

326. Jones, *California*, 38–39.

327. Ibid.

328. "Dice and Marbles," *Sacramento Daily Union*, November 20, 1860.

329. "Gambling," *Sacramento Daily Union*, April 13, 1854.

330. Colville, *City Directory of Sacramento*, 11.

331. "Fight at a Fancy Ball," *Daily Democratic State Journal*, July 12, 1855.

332. "Sacramento Lyceum," *California Statesman*, December 8, 1854.

333. "Lyceum," *Daily Democratic State Journal*, November 3, 1854.

334. "Lyceum," *Daily Democratic State Journal*, December 29, 1855.

335. "The Lyceum," *Daily Democratic State Journal*, February 11, 1855.

336. "Suwanee House," *Daily Democratic State Journal*, October 1, 1853; "A Literary Society," *Sacramento Daily Union*, January 5, 1854.

337. "National Amphitheater," *Daily Democratic State Journal*, August 16, 1856.

338. "Bull Fight," *Daily Democratic State Journal*, December 21, 1854

339. "Dog Fights," *Daily Democratic State Journal*, August 15, 1856.

340. "Badger Baiting," *Sacramento Daily Union*, December 15, 1858.

341. "The Engine Race," *Daily Democratic State Journal*, May 27, 1857.

342. "Hydrant Saloon," *Daily Democratic State Journal*, August 5, 1854.

343. "Disgusting," *Daily Democratic State Journal*, September 6, 1855.

344. Hall, *Old Sacramento*, 66.

345. "Jimmy," *Daily Democratic State Journal*, July 21, 1856.

Chapter 5

346. "Jocko," *Daily Democratic State Journal*, January 24, 1857.

347. "Cold Water Army," *Daily Democratic State Journal*, December 8, 1856.

348. "Anti-Swearing Society," *Daily Democratic State Journal*, January 10, 1857; "Anti-Swearing Society," *Daily Democratic State Journal*, February 3, 1857.

349. California State Legislature, "An Act to Provide for the Better Observance of the Sabbath," 124–25.

350. "Sunday Cases," *Sacramento Daily Union*, June 21, 1858.

351. "Sunday Law," *Sacramento Daily Union*, June 8, 1858.

352. Blakely, *American State Papers*, 166.

353. "Liquid Manufacturers," *Sacramento Daily Union*, January 2, 1859.

354. "Ohio Brewery," *Sacramento Daily Union*, August 27, 1860.

355. "Rablin's Tiger Ale," *Daily Democratic State Journal*, March 31, 1857.

356. "Rablin's Tiger Ale," *Daily Democratic State Journal*, March 15, 1857.

357. "Sacramento Ale and Porter," *Sacramento Daily Union*, May 24, 1859.

358. "Green's Exchange," *Daily Democratic State Journal*, August 19, 1853.

359. "Phoenix Brewery," *Sacramento Daily Union*, January 4, 1858.

360. "A Glass of Lager," *Sacramento Daily Union*, July 20, 1858.

361. "Accidental Shooting," *Sacramento Daily Union*, April 17, 1858.

362. "Died," *Sacramento Daily Union*, November 9, 1859.

363. "Inquest on the Body of Maria Rupp," *Sacramento Daily Union*, November 20, 1857.

364. Ibid.

365. Ibid.

366. "The Dead," *Sacramento Daily Union*, November 21, 1857.

367. "Metz, the Murderer," *Sacramento Daily Union*, October 3, 1858.

368. "Violation of City Ordinance," *Daily Democratic State Journal*, November 27, 1856.

369. Ibid.

370. Ibid.

371. "Charivari No. 2," *Sacramento Daily Union*, November 26, 1860.

372. "Body Found," *Sacramento Daily Union*, March 28, 1861.

373. "Accident from Burning Fluid," *Sacramento Daily Union*, July 28, 1857.

374. "For Frazier River," *Sacramento Daily Union*, May 25, 1858.

375. Kennedy, *Agriculture of the United States*, 12; "Foreign vs. Home Wines," *Sacramento Daily Union*, December 16, 1853.

376. "Two Hours at Smith's," *Sacramento Daily Union*, August 6, 1860.

377. Ibid.

378. "Grape Arbor," *Sacramento Daily Union*, July 18, 1860.

379. "Muscat Grapes," *Sacramento Daily Union*, September 7, 1858.

380. "Choice Grapes," *Sacramento Daily Union*, September 10, 1861.

381. "Native Wine," *Sacramento Daily Union*, August 13, 1859.

382. Ibid.

383. "Anaconda at Large," *Sacramento Daily Union*, June 27, 1859; "The Anaconda," *Sacramento Daily Union*, June 28, 1859.

384. "Native Born," *Daily Democratic State Journal*, July 15, 1855.

385. "Grand Oyster Supper," *Sacramento Daily Union*, December 2, 1857.

386. "New Sazerac Building," *Sacramento Daily Union*, July 21, 1858.

387. "Assault and Battery," *Sacramento Daily Union*, October 13, 1858.

388. "Sazerac Saloon," *Sacramento Daily Union*, December 11, 1860.

389. Erdoes, *Saloons*, 118.

390. "The Pearl," *Daily Democratic State Journal*, January 7, 1855.

CHAPTER 6

391. "The Flag," *Sacramento Daily Union*, August 11, 1861.

392. This was likely the First Battle of Bull Run, taking place on July 21, 1861, when Union troops under the command of General Irvin McDowell attacked Confederate regulars at Manassas Junction. Despite initial successes for the Union side, the Rebels recovered and sent the Union attackers retreating back toward Washington, D.C.

393. William Carr, "Civil War Welded California into Solid, Mature State," *Sacramento Bee*, April 23, 1961.

394. Wright, *History of Sacramento County*, 332.

395. "The Green Ribbon," *Sacramento Daily Union*, July 21, 1861.

396. "Secession Flag," *Sacramento Daily Union*, July 6, 1861.

397. "Fireworks in the Event," *Sacramento Daily Union*, July 6, 1861.

398. "Sacramento Had Her Johnny Rebs, Too," *Sacramento Daily Union*, July 1, 1956.

399. "Not Quite a Duel," *Sacramento Daily Union*, May 2, 1861.

400. Lehr, *Sutterville*, 89.

401. "Row at Sutterville," *Sacramento Daily Union*, December 14, 1861.

BIBLIOGRAPHY

NEWSPAPERS

California Alta
California Statesman
Daily Democratic State Journal
Illustrated London News
New York Daily Times
New York Tribune
Placer Times
Sacramento Bee
Sacramento Daily Union
Sacramento Transcript
San Francisco Morning Call

MONOGRAPHS AND REMINISCENCES

Bancroft, Hubert Howe. *History of California*. San Francisco: The History Co., 1886–90.

Bell, Horace. *Reminiscences of a Ranger: Early Times in Southern California*. Norman: University of Oklahoma Press, 1999.

Blakely, William Addison. *American State Papers Bearing on Sunday Legislation: Legislative, Executive, Judicial*. Washington, D.C.: Religious Liberty Association, 1911.

Boessenecker, John. *Gold Dust and Gunsmoke: Tales of Gold Rush Outlaws, Gunfighters, Lawmen, and Vigilantes*. Hoboken, NJ: John Wiley & Sons, 1999.

Borthwick, John David. *The Gold Hunters: A First-Hand Picture of Life in California Mining Camps in the Early Fifties*. Edited by Horace Kephart. Cleveland, OH: International Fiction Library, 1917.

Bosker, Gideon. *Bowled Over: A Roll Down Memory Lane*. San Francisco: Chronicle Books, 2002.

Brannan, Samuel. *Scoundrel's Tale: The Samuel Brannan Papers*. Edited by Will Bagley. Spokane, WA: Arthur H. Clark, 1999.

Canfield, Chauncey L. *Diary of a Forty-Niner*. New York: Turtle Point Press, 1992.

Collins, Laura T. *Sutter's Fort*. Sacramento, CA: Larkin Printing Company, 1939.

Colville, Samuel. *City Directory of Sacramento*. San Francisco: Monson & Valentine Book & Job Printers, 1854.

Culver, J. Horace. *Sacramento City Directory, 1851*. Sacramento, CA: California State Library Foundation, 2000.

DeArment, Robert. *Knights of the Green Cloth: The Saga of the Frontier Gamblers*. Norman: University of Oklahoma Press, 1982.

Decker, Peter. *The Diaries of Peter Decker: Overland to California in 1849 and Life in the Mines, 1850–1851*. Edited by H.S. Giffen. Georgetown, CA: Talisman Press, 1966.

de Rutte, Theophile. *The Adventures of a Young Swiss in California: The Gold Rush Account of Theophile de Rutte*. Translated and edited by Mary Grace Paquette. Sacramento, CA: Sacramento Book Collectors Club, 1992.

Eifler, Mark. *Gold Rush Capitalists: Greed and Growth in Sacramento*. Albuquerque: University of New Mexico Press, 2002.

Erdoes, Richard. *Saloons of the Old West*. New York: Knopf, 1979.

Findlay, John M. *People of Chance: Gambling in American Society from Jamestown to Las Vegas*. New York: Oxford University Press, 1986.

Gerstäcker, Friedrich. *California Gold Mines*. Oakland, CA: Biobooks, 1946.

Grimshaw, William Robinson. *Grimshaw's Narrative: Being the Story of Life and Events in California During Flush Times, Particularly the Years 1848–1850. Including a Biographical Sketch*. Edited by J.R.K. Kantor. Sacramento, CA: Sacramento Book Collector's Club, 1964.

Hayes, Peter J. *The Lower American River: Prehistory to Parkway*. Carmichael, CA: American River Natural History Association, 2005.

Holden, William M. *Sacramento: Excursions into Its History and Natural World*. Fair Oaks, CA: Two Rivers Publication Company, 1988.

Holladay, J.S. *The World Rushed In: The California Gold Rush Experience*. New York: Simon and Schuster, 1983.

Howe, Octavius Thorndike. *Argonauts of '49*. Cambridge, MA: Harvard University Press, 1923.

Hume, Charles. "The Eagle Theater" in *Sketches of Old Sacramento*. Sacramento, CA: Sacramento County Historical Society, 1976.

Johnston, William G. *Experiences of a Forty-Niner*. New York: Arno Press, 1973.

Jones, Thomas R. *California in the Days of Gold*. Los Angeles: House of Asdit, 1931.

Leach, Frank. *Recollections of a Newspaperman: A Record of Life and Events in California*. San Francisco: S. Levinson, 1917.

Lehr, Ernest E. *Sutterville: The Unsuccessful Attempt to Establish a Town Safe from Floods*. Sacramento: California State University–Sacramento, 1958.

Lienhard, Heinrich. *A Pioneer at Sutter's Fort: The Adventures of Heinrich Lienhard*. Los Angeles: Calafia Press, 1941.

Loosely, Allyn. *Foreign Born Population of California, 1848–1920*. San Francisco: R&R Research, 1971.

Lord, Israel Shipman Pelton. *At the Extremity of Civilization: A Meticulously Descriptive Diary of an Illinois Physician's Journey in 1849 Along the Oregon Trail to the Goldmines and Cholera of California, Thence in Two Years to Return by Boat via Panama*. Jefferson, NC: McFarland and Co., 1995.

Morse, John Frederick. *First History of Sacramento City*. Sacramento, CA: Sacramento Book Collector's Club, 1945.

Olson, William H. *Archeological Investigations at Sutter's Fort State Historical Monument, 1959*. Sacramento: California Department of Natural Resources, Division of Beaches and Parks, Interpretive Services, 1961.

Ryan, William Redmond. *Personal Adventures in Upper and Lower California in 1848–9*. London: Parry, 1852.

Sacramento Bee. *Sacramento Guide Book*. Sacramento, CA: Sacramento Bee, 1939.

Sacramento Genealogical Society. *Women Proprietors or Sole Traders: Sacramento, California, 1850–1930*. Citrus Heights, CA: Root Cellar, n.d.

Schoonover, Thomas J. *The Life and Times of Gen'l John A. Sutter*. Sacramento, CA: D. Johnston & Co., 1895.

Secrest, William. *Blood and Honor*. Fresno, CA: Saga-West Publishing, 1970.

Taylor, Bayard. *Eldorado; or, Adventures in the Path of Empire: Comprising a Voyage to California, via Panama; Life in San Francisco and Monterey; Pictures of the Gold Region and Experiences of Mexican Travel*. Glorieta, NM: Rio Grande Press, 1967.

Thrapp, Dan L. *Encyclopedia of Frontier Biography*. Spokane, WA: Arthur H. Clark Company, 1990.

Wells, Evelyn, and Harry C. Peterson. *The '49ers*. Garden City, NY: Doubleday, 1949.

Wright, George F., ed. *History of Sacramento County, California: With Illustrations Descriptive of Its Scenery, Residences, Public Buildings, Fine Blocks and Manufactories from Original Sketches by Artists of the Highest Ability*. Oakland, CA: Thompson and West, 1880.

Wyman, Walker D. "Sacramento Booms" in *California Emigrant Letters*. New York: AMS Press, 1973.

Scholarly Articles

Caesar, Clarence. "The Historical Demographics of Sacramento's Black Community, 1848–1900." *California History* 75, no. 3 (Fall 1996): 198–213.

Childress, Diana. "From Wet to Dry." *Cobblestone* 14, no. 8 (October 1993): 4.

Davis, W.N. "Research Use of County Court Records, 1850–1879, and Incidental Intimate Glimpses of California Life and Society, Part I." *California Historical Quarterly* 52, no. 3 (Fall 1973): 241–66.

de Massey, Ernest. "A Frenchman in the Gold Rush." Translated by Marguerite Eyer. *California Historical Society Quarterly* 5, no. 4 (December 1926): 342–77.

Hamilton, Gary G. "Adventurism and the California Gold Rush." *American Journal of Sociology* 83, no. 6 (May 1978): 1,466–90.

Johnson, David. "Vigilance and the Law: The Moral Authority of Popular Justice in the Far West." *American Quarterly* 33, no. 5 (Winter 1981): 558–86.

Kirker, Harold. "El Dorado Gothic: Gold Rush Architects and Architecture." *California Historical Society Quarterly* 38, no. 1 (March 1959): 31–46.

Lapp, Rudolph. "The Negro in Gold Rush California." *Journal of Negro History* 49, no. 2 (April 1964): 81–98.

Simpson, Alice Fisher. "Sacramento's Historic Buildings." *Golden Notes* 1, no. 2 (October 1954): 1–8.

Tinling, Marion. "Bloomerism Comes to California." *California History* 61, no. 1 (Spring 1982): 18–25.

West, Elliott. "The Saloon: A Frontier Institution." *American West* 17, no. 1 (1980): 14–29.

Wright, Doris. "The Making of Cosmopolitan California, Part I." *California Historical Society Quarterly* 19, no. 4 (December 1940): 323–43.

———. "The Making of Cosmopolitan California, Part II." *California Historical Society Quarterly* 20, no. 1 (March 1941): 65–79.

Government Documents

Ancestry.com. "1850 United States Federal Census." Ancestry.com Operations Inc., 2009.

———. "1860 United States Federal Census." Ancestry.com Operations Inc., 2009.

California State Legislature. "An Act to License Gaming." Sacramento: California State Printing Office, 1851.

———. "An Act to Prohibit the Collection of Accounts for Liquors Sold at Retail." Sacramento: California State Printing Office, 1858.

———. "An Act to Provide for the Better Observance of the Sabbath." Sacramento: California State Printing Office, 1858.

———. "An Act to Suppress Gaming." Sacramento: California State Printing Office, 1855.

———. "An Act to Take the Sense of the People of This State, at the General Election in A.D. 1855, on the Passage of a Prohibitory Liquor Law." Sacramento: California State Printing Office, 1855.

Hall, Carroll D. *Old Sacramento: A Report on Its Significance to the City, State and Nation, with Recommendations for the Preservation and Use of Its Principal Historical Structures and Sites, Part II.* Sacramento: California Department of Natural Resources, Division of Beaches and Parks, 1958.

Kennedy, Joseph C.G. *Agriculture of the United States in 1860; Compiled from the Original Returns of the Eighth Census, Under the Direction of the Secretary of the Interior.* Washington, D.C.: Government Printing Office, 1864.

Sacramento Court of First Magistrate. *J. Brown v. Hubbard, Brown and Company* (Eagle Theater Bankruptcy Case). Civil Case No. 209 (October 28, 1849).

———. *Jones and Brown v. Z. Hubbard, Brown and Company* (Eagle Theater Bankruptcy Case). Civil Case No. 222, (November 6, 1849).

———. *Jones, Brown et al v. Z. Hubbard, Brown and Company* (Eagle Theater Bankruptcy Case). Civil Case No. 188 (October 29, 1849).

Sacramento Probate Court. "Estate of Peter Slater." Sacramento County, CA, No. 6.

INDEX

ABOUT THE AUTHOR

James Scott has been a reference librarian at the Sacramento Public Library since 2000. In his time at SPL, he has authored, with colleague Tom Tolley, three books on local Sacramento history. He holds a bachelor's degree in history and political science from Marquette University, as well as master's degrees in European history and library and information science. He and his family live in Sacramento.

Set in the original 1917 Carnegie Foundation–funded section of the Sacramento Public Library, the Sacramento Room was founded in 1995 as an archives and special collection for primary and secondary research materials relative to the history of Sacramento city and county. Its rare book, book art, map, city directory, photograph, digital and manuscript

Sacramento Room. *Sacramento Public Library.*

collections make it one of the premier spots for historical research in Northern California. The Sacramento Room can be visited online at www. saclibrary.org/Locations/Sacramento-Room.